MALIBU BURNING

MWC Press
30765 Pacific Coast Highway #141
Malibu, CA 90265

www.mwcpress.com
Printed in the United States of America

First Printing, 2019

ISBN 978-1-7334705-0-6 (paperback)
ISBN 978-1-7334705-1-3 (ebook)
ISBN 978-1-7334705-2-0 (audiobook)
ISBN 978-1-7334705-3-7 (hardcover)

Erin,
Thank you for all you've done!

MALIBU BURNING

The Real Story Behind LA's Most Devastating Wildfire

rkerbeck@me.com

Robert Kerbeck

FIRE HISTORY MAP

Woolsey Incident
CA-VNC-91023
November 19, 2018
Final Acres - 96,949

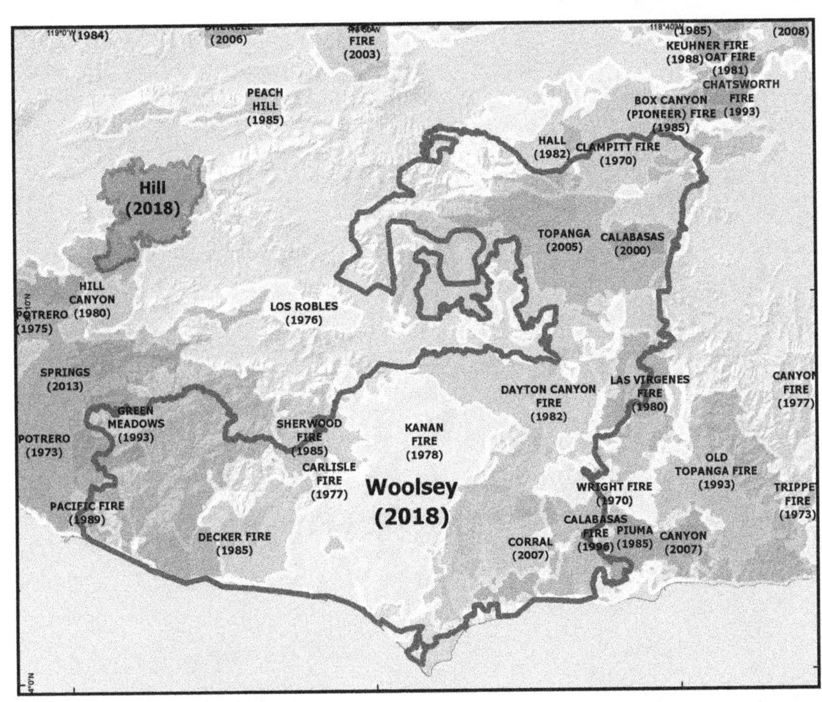

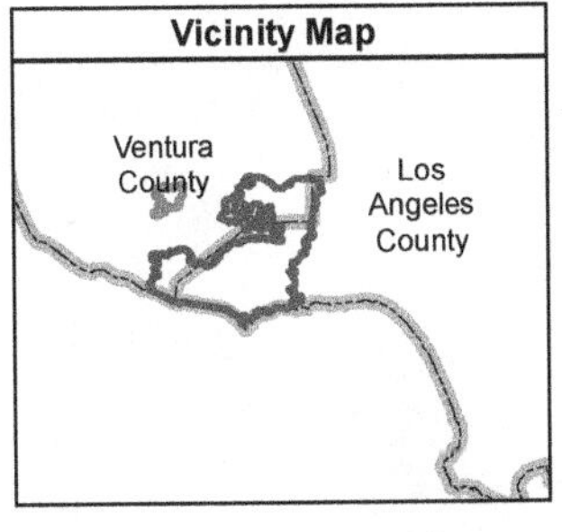

Fire History 1970 to Present

- 1970-1979
- 1980-1989
- 1900-1999
- 2000-Present
- Hill Fire 2018
- Woolsey Fire Perimeter

1:125,000
NAD 83

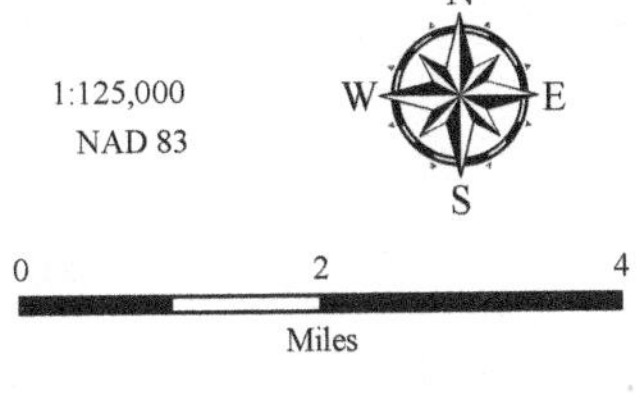

"I think we have to reach a tipping point. If we don't, I worry we'll treat these mass burnings like we treat mass shootings. We'll think about it for a day, and then move on. Not really addressing it."

—Stephen Pyne, a native Californian and professor of history at Arizona State University

"In Malibu, things do not remain the same for very long."

—Dorothy Stotsenberg, My Fifty Years in Malibu

CONTENTS

Gardia spraying our house with Phos-Chek as the fire approached.
PHOTO ROBERT KERBECK

PROLOGUE

THE ACCIDENTAL FIREFIGHTERS

Few things in this world will forever change you like the terror of thinking you're about to be burned alive in front of your kid. But at 11:44 on the morning of Friday, November 9, as the flames of the Woolsey Fire barreled across our yard, I was gutted by the possibility. The fire had been burning since the day before, but all at once it crashed down into my Malibu Park neighborhood, and somehow there were more children fighting the blaze than there were firefighters. My sixteen-year-old, Davis, was one of them. Garden hoses in hand, legs braced against the searing winds, he and I were pushing the very edge of judgment and safety in our desperation to protect our home. As fireballs pelted the yard around us, it hit me that I'd made a horrific mistake.

Teaching risk assessment was one of the most important jobs of a parent, and I was imparting this lesson to my son in the worst possible way.

My wife, Gardia, jumped into her car and ripped out of the driveway. She'd known from the beginning. She'd sensed the danger in a way I hadn't. That morning, she was up at six o'clock tracking the fires on the other side of the Santa Monica Mountains as well as the extreme Santa Ana winds in the forecast. Known as "devil winds," Santa Anas blow in hot and dry from the desert and pick up speed in the canyons and arroyos of Southern California until they hit

Malibu with hurricane force. At best, these winds are an annoyance, creating itchy skin and short tempers. In fire season, however, they are life-threatening.

By the time Gardia received confirmation that the fire had hopped the 101 Freeway, the last major firebreak before it would plow into western Malibu where we live, she'd woken up Davis and put him to work packing family photos and videos.

I was still asleep when the mandatory evacuation order came by phone call, text, and email at 7:30 a.m. I'd popped up, thrown on a pair of jeans, and hustled to the toolshed that served as my home office to get the only possession that mattered to me: my laptop.

By the time I came back out into the sun, the smoke was already throwing a low scrim across the sky. I could smell it, feel it on my skin.

I grabbed Davis and a couple of garden hoses, and we started watering down the foliage in front of our all-wood Victorian home. Davis had spent his whole life there. We'd bought it in 2000 during a rare lull in the housing market. The height notches on the kitchen wall. The swing set and sliding board in the backyard. My late father's piano in the living room. We damn sure were going to give the place a fighting chance.

Within half an hour, the sky had gone from grayish to black, though over the ocean to the south I could still see a stretch of blue. The severity of these signs convinced me that more serious measures were required. So I jogged into the garage and dragged out the fire pump.

A surfer buddy, Tim, once told me what gear to buy for the inevitable wildfire. A lifelong local, Tim had also warned me that there would be no firefighters when the time came, that if I wanted to save my place I would need to stay and fight for it myself. Being from Philadelphia, I couldn't imagine firefighters not showing up. I wasn't sure I believed him, but it couldn't hurt to be prepared. He explained that the hydrant water would run out, so it was essential that I have a pump and my own water source. I glanced toward our hot tub and hoped it would be enough.

I wheeled the pump down toward it and attached the fire hose while Davis drenched the house. I risked a look around. Many of our neighbors had highly flammable eucalyptus and pine trees on their properties. Some had entire groves, with individual trunks extending more than a hundred feet high. Everywhere around me, the brush was dry and brittle. California had been in drought conditions regularly since 2012, and suddenly everything looked like kindling.

I yanked the cord and the pump's engine sputtered on. When Davis was little, testing the pump was the highlight of summer. Blasting water hundreds of feet in the air from a fire hose was, to us, the definition of a good time. As much fun as it was, I could never get out of my mind that one day we might have to use the pump for its true purpose. And that my only child might be operating that hose.

I increased the idle and braced for the water pressure. But there was none. The engine ran, but the pump wasn't pulling water out of the spa. I shut it off and started it again. Still nothing.

My wife is the repair person in the family, so I ran to the house to get her. But she couldn't figure out the problem either. Frustrated, we stood in the yard and looked skyward. The dark, smudgy air seemed to have lightened, as if the sun had come out after a rainstorm. On the ridge above us, an orange glow pulsed.

"Get the Phos-Chek," Gardia said, pointing to the garage. "Take the hose up to the hydrant."

Over the years I'd acquired other gear: Masks, nozzles, a specialized wrench to access the hydrant at the top of our driveway, and a flame-retardant chemical called Phos-Chek. But I'd never used any of it. And as I grabbed the wrench and chugged to the hydrant I realized I didn't know what to do with it.

"Unscrew the cap," Gardia said, arriving seconds behind me. "Then attach the hose."

I followed her instructions but still had no idea how the thing turned on.

"Use the wrench now." She pointed at a bolt I'd missed. "Lefty loosey," she added before I went too far in the wrong direction. I yanked the wrench the other way and immediately the hose flushed with water.

"Where'd you learn that?" I asked.

"YouTube," she said. "Last night."

I wanted to hug her, but a change in the ridgeline drew our attention. Fire was pouring over it the way water was flowing out of the hose. It was no more than a third of a mile from our house.

"Come on, get the Phos-Chek," she shouted.

In the garage, I grabbed the giant blue jug that had sat untouched for years. I poured a bunch of the liquid into the canister that we'd attached to the fire hose. Gardia turned on the nozzle and blasted our house with foamy water while I rejoined Davis to keep wetting down the grounds with garden hoses. In that moment, the three of us moving in sync—Gardia sweeping the fluming spray back and forth across the siding and windows, Davis arcing water onto the plants, my own spray attacking the trees—I felt a surge of pride and exhilaration. We were doing it. Together. We were going to beat this thing. My family was kicking ass.

That's when the fire left the ridgeline and lunged at us. It didn't crawl or creep down the hillside, didn't roll forward in a fluid motion. It flew, the flames accelerated by the super-heated Santa Ana winds. One moment it was up there, the next it was right fucking next to us. It may as well have teleported.

"We gotta go," Gardia shouted. She dragged the heavy hose down the driveway behind her, dousing every last inch of the house as she ran. She dropped it and jumped into her car. *Go go go go go*, I yelled to her in my head.

I threw my hose down next to Davis, and fire exploded onto the ground between us as if it had been thrown. In seconds, we were in my car ready to follow Gardia. Through the windshield, I saw that I'd left the garden hose on. A sprinkler once broke on our property, and the water bill was astronomical. Only later would I be able to take the full measure of my stupidity. But in the moment, Davis mute with confusion beside me, I jumped out of the car and started toward the driveway to turn off the water.

Embers and debris bombarded me before I could go ten feet. The blistering force of the wind nearly knocked me over, and I could feel my balance slip, the hairs on my forearm crackling along my skin. I bent to turn off the water and in a whoosh, like a blazing genie materializing from a giant lamp, a tornado made of fire appeared in front of me. At the far edge of the burning world, I heard my son scream, "Dad!"

And that was when I knew he was going to watch me die.

Tucking instinctively, I felt the flames whisk above me without touching down. I only avoided catching fire because I happened to be so low to the ground. In a half-crawl, I made my way toward Davis without looking back.

I was in the car and about to drive off when something cracked above us. We looked up to see a power pole falling. It missed the car by mere feet. I pulled forward and carefully maneuvered around the wires dangling overhead.

Even in my stunned daze I knew we were doing the worst thing you could do in a wildfire, which was to evacuate in the midst of the firestorm. We should have taken shelter inside our house until it passed, then knocked down the spot fires on the property. We'd also gotten into a car. If we got trapped, we would burn to death. But I knew if we could make it to Zuma Beach, only minutes away, we'd be safe—the water wasn't going to burn, or the sand, or the asphalt parking lot.

And anyway, that's where Gardia was. My wife. I had to bring her son to her, unscathed.

I drove down the hill in shock and pulled into the parking lot at Zuma, just on the other side of the Pacific Coast Highway. Davis and I slowly emerged from the car to survey the scene. The lot was packed with the vehicles of those who'd fled the fire. Horses and other large animals stood among the cars. Llamas were tied to lifeguard towers. An elderly man stumbled by, moaning. His face seemed to have been melted by the flames. People wandered around looking lost, as if they'd forgotten where they parked their cars. It was a waking nightmare, humans processing disaster in real time.

Tim turned out to have been right. No firefighters had showed up at my home. Or on my street. Or in my neighborhood.

I found Gardia and told her and Davis to wait in the cars while I went looking for firefighters. But as I moved west across the lot, the smoke grew thicker. I'd left my mask in the car and thought about going back but figured I could handle the discomfort. I was wrong. My eyes began to water, and I started to cough. The air itself burned. Soon I was hacking and couldn't breathe. Eventually, it was too much and I turned back, stumbling, then running to the relative safety of the car.

Through the haze, I finally caught my first glimpse of those officially tasked with fighting the fire. Gathered on the blacktop was a group of firefighters standing by a quintet of idling engines, seemingly waiting to be told where to go. If only they had turned to the mountains over their shoulders they would've seen what the rest of us had already fought to survive: beneath a thick, drifting black cloak of ash as long as the sky, the hillsides and canyons of Malibu were being eaten alive by fire.

Our home standing amidst the smoke and wreckage of our neighborhood.

PHOTO MATT SAVER

The burned gate, truck, and home of my neighbor.

PHOTO ROBERT KERBECK

1

FRONTIER DAYS

The Woolsey Fire, which burst alive in the mountains above Malibu in the early morning on Friday, November 9, 2018, turned out to be the worst fire LA County has ever seen and one of the most destructive blazes in California history. The fire burned 100,000 acres, forced more than 250,000 people to evacuate, cost $6 billion, and killed three people. It's some kind of miracle that the number is that low given the speed, reach, and aggression of the fire and the initial lack of firefighting support. But even so, tens of thousands suffered smoke inhalation from the toxic soot and ash, putting them at risk of complicated, long-lasting heath issues. Animals in the area, of which there are many, domesticated and wild, suffered far greater losses. Nearly 2,000 homes and structures were lost. In my neighborhood of 275 houses, approximately 180 were destroyed, and seventeen of nineteen homes on my street alone burned to the ground.

Ours was one of the few to survive.

At the time the fire advanced on my house, there wasn't a single fire engine on site, let alone planes or helicopters dropping water or fire-retardant chemicals. Resources were spread thin, and the state of California was being tested as never before. Two days earlier, there'd been a mass shooting at the Borderline Bar in nearby Thousand Oaks. Twelve people were murdered. That site was only minutes from where the Woolsey Fire started. A second fire, the Hill Fire, was also burning nearby. At the same time, the Camp Fire further north was decimating the town of Paradise.

The stories of those who survived that test—and those who failed—illustrate one of the central misconceptions about Malibu and the 13,000 people who live there. They are not, for the most part, rich *or* famous. There is a whole social structure in Malibu that most outsiders don't even know exists. For every Barbra Streisand zealously guarding her cliffside estate, there are scores of residents who struggle to make ends meet. These men and women—teachers, working couples, broke surfers, students, families with kids, the elderly living on fixed incomes—banded together during the Woolsey Fire to save hundreds of homes, sometimes entire neighborhoods.

In a number of cases, firefighters refused to fight the fire. Water often ran low and then sometimes ran out. A couple in their mid-eighties used buckets to save their home and other homes nearby. Children manned hoses. And, every once in a while, a celebrity pitched in. If not for the heroic actions of these individuals, Malibu would have been completely decimated.

Still, for all its destruction, the Woolsey Fire wasn't unusual. Fall is fire season in Malibu. Wildfires have been periodically raging up and down the coast since the first recorded one in the early 1800s.

My family had already had small tastes of fire and nature's devastating potential. Not long after Gardia and I moved into our home in 2000, the Santa Anas alone destroyed our gazebo and snapped a flagpole in half. And we had a brush fire on the hillside above our house almost exactly a year before the Woolsey blaze, in late 2017. On that December day, I'd been writing in the tool shed when I heard honking. A truck was speeding back and forth on my street.

"Fire," the driver yelled. "Get out of here!"

I emerged and saw a small fire on the street above ours. The Santa Anas hurled flaming tumbleweeds toward me, and just like that another section of the hill caught fire, this one closer. Gardia ran inside to pack valuables while

Davis and I grabbed garden hoses and began watering the house. I wanted to get out the fire pump but there wasn't time. The fire was practically on our street. I remembered my surfer buddy Tim's warning about the lack of firefighters, and as the brush fire crept down the hillside, I prayed he was wrong.

Over the shrieking wind, I suddenly heard a siren. Less than a minute later, two engines pulled up and began to fight the fire. I heard a rumble in the distance and glanced up to see a helicopter swooping in. When it was over the flames, it released a deluge of water, dousing them completely. Davis and I might have cheered if we thought the firefighters could hear us. I couldn't believe the fire had come so close and that we were rescued at the last moment. The entire event had taken less than half an hour.

That experience explains why, as the Woolsey Fire approached, I was thinking I might sleep through it. By then I had learned that while many residents left right away when they received the evacuation notices, most longtime Malibuites did not. After all, no one is going to force you to leave your home, let alone arrest you if you don't.

But the hard truth is that by late morning on the day the Woolsey Fire attacked my home, I'd come obscenely close to being killed along with my son. And for what? A house? I hadn't packed a single personal item, so it's not as if objects and possessions mattered much to me. It was more that I loved our home, as if it too, were a part of our family, and I wanted to give it a chance to survive.

It's hard to explain to people why you would ever take such a risk. But I've come to believe that the key to understanding why Gardia, Davis, and I, along with so many others, decided to stay behind to fight a massive wildfire is this: today's Malibu isn't that far removed from the frontier it was a hundred years ago.

One of the last links to Malibu's Wild West days, Millie Decker, died only a month after the Woolsey Fire at the age of ninety-eight. Millie's husband, Jimmy, was a descendant of Marion Decker, the first Decker to settle in the hills above what the Spanish had named Rancho Topanga Malibu Sequit. Over the years, the area became known as Rancho Malibu and then just Malibu—or if you were new in town and thought yourself cute, "The 'Bu."

Marion Decker came to the area in the late 1800s as a homesteader. The Homestead Act of 1862 guaranteed 160 acres to anyone who made a claim on open land, then built a house, planted crops, and lived there for five years. Marion and his descendants never left. Millie's ranch, located in the northwest corner of today's Malibu, is all that remains of Marion's original land parcel in a canyon now named after the family: Decker Canyon.

The Woolsey Fire marked the first time Millie was ever evacuated. As a child, when a blaze would come through the fire-prone canyon, she filled the water barrels scattered around the property. She would hike through heavy brush in search of creeks, fill her buckets, and lug them back in the hot, dry Santa Ana conditions. Family members would then wet burlap gunnysacks and whack them against the fires. The combination of the wetness and the force of the slap was usually enough to put out the flames, or at least prevent them from getting too big, always the key to protecting your home. Millie fought numerous fires during a lifetime that spanned nearly a century and not once had her house burned.

The other family most associated with Malibu is the Rindges. As an example of how connected Malibu still is to those early days, the Rindges were listed in the paperwork when Gardia and I bought our home in 2000 since they had once owned our land.

If the Deckers were examples of hardscrabble Westerners who lived off the land, Frederick Rindge and his wife, Mae, were the opposite: New Englanders with a taste for luxury. Frederick was a wealthy Bostonian who had attended Harvard with Teddy Roosevelt. He wanted the perfect paradise in which to live and raise his family, and discovered it in the former home of the Chumash, the Native peoples who'd lived in the area from approximately 500 BC. The "Sequit" in Malibu's original name comes from the name of the largest Chumash village in the area, now known as Leo Carrillo State Park, about five miles west of Zuma Beach and Point Dume. Artifacts and burial grounds of the Chumash are discovered in Malibu to this day.

The Chumash began to be displaced from their home in 1802, when the Spanish granted the Rancho Malibu parcel to Jose Bartolome Tapia, who was part of an earlier expedition to California. The Tapias used the land for grazing cattle, and in 1848 a Frenchman, Leon Victor Prudhomme, bought it from Tapia's widow for 400 pesos—200 in cash—the remainder in groceries and wine. Prudhomme didn't last long. He sold the 13,000-acre property for 10 cents an acre to Matthew Keller, an Irishman with a penchant for winemaking. Keller's wines were the first California wines to be sold on the East Coast. His name was also listed in the papers Gardia and I signed when we purchased our home. When Keller died in 1881, his son Henry took over. And in 1892, Henry sold the entire parcel to Frederick Rindge for $10 an acre.

In 1893, Rindge began building a home for his family. It was a Victorian like ours, and constructing it was a tremendous challenge since there were no roads. All supplies had to be brought in twenty miles from Santa Monica on horseback or by wagon at low tide via the hard sand of the beach. A tide log told the workers when they could go and when to return.

Land is at a premium in Malibu today, but even back then it was contentious. The shortcut homesteaders like Marion Decker took to get into and back from Santa Monica for supplies was on Rindge's property. At first, the two men got along. They even collaborated to improve the path into town, which benefitted them both. Rindge paid for the men and the material; Decker supervised the work.

But in 1895, Rindge put up locked gates at Las Flores Canyon to prevent squatters and trespassers from entering his private Malibu. (Gates like these exist today in the Point Dume area to prevent outsiders from surfing the waves there.) Rindge staffed his gates with armed guards on horseback—Point Dume hasn't quite resorted to this yet—and gave keys to the homesteaders, explaining that he had no intention of preventing the families from accessing the road.

But Decker discovered that if he and the homesteaders agreed to the arrangement and the gates stood for five years, Rindge could claim the road as his private property. If the mood struck him—or any of his descendants—Rindge could deny the homesteaders the easement. Taking the treacherous mountain passes would then be the only way for homesteaders to reach their land from Santa Monica. This put the men at odds and into the courts for what would become a decades-long battle over the road, which eventually became the Pacific Coast Highway.

Rindge published a book about the beauty of his new home called *Happy Days in Southern California.* In it, he wrote about his fear of fire and the dreaded Santa Anas, which he branded "death winds." In 1903, the Rindge family had its own brush with a wildfire when the coast was engulfed by a wall of flames that stretched the thirty miles from Santa Monica to the Ventura County line. The Rindges were at their home in Santa Monica when the fire occurred, and their foreman was unable to save the Victorian. All that was left was the chimney and a scorched moonscape that Malibuites, past and present, are all too familiar with. The source of the blaze remained a mystery, but the bad blood with the homesteaders left the Rindges convinced that the fire had been set as an act of revenge.

Frederick Rindge died suddenly in 1905, putting his wife, Mae, in charge. Over the next thirty-five years, her efforts to protect Frederick's private Malibu, which still had turtles in Santa Monica Bay, would go all the way to the Supreme Court. To fund her legal battles—and prevent highways and railroads from going through her property—Mae made a decision that would change Malibu forever.

In 1927, she began leasing lots in an attempt to stave off bankruptcy. A realtor had told her how much money she could make by selling, but the idea of *permanent* neighbors was unpalatable to Mae. She leased the lots to the people who had the most money at the time—silent movie actors. The first was a Swedish actress named Anna Q. Nilsson, who predated Greta Garbo and Ingrid Bergman. To attract even more of this wealthy sector of society, Mae created the Malibu Motion Picture Colony, a small strip of beach that would become known as the Malibu Colony. Soon, dozens of movie stars, directors, writers, and producers were living on the beach.

Although the majority of people who live in Malibu today aren't high-profile Hollywood types, its reputation as a celebrity enclave started there.

And it all began with a wildfire.

The dots indicate homes lost in my Malibu Park neighborhood.

Welcome to Corral Canyon sign

PHOTO PAUL MORRA

2

ENGINE 271

Paul Morra looks like the actor Paul Rudd and lives in the upper part of Malibu's Corral Canyon, an area known as the Malibu Bowl. Directly below his community is the El Nido neighborhood. Together the two areas make up the 220 homes in Corral Canyon. Though the communities are minutes from the ocean, the road to reach them is steep and filled with tight turns. El Nido translates as "The Nest." The Malibu Bowl is another 500 feet up on the hillside.

Morra started building his home in 2006 after a six-year process to get the permits. By mid-2007, he and his wife, Danielle, were ready to celebrate. Not only were they moving into their new home, they were having twins due that November.

But on July 4, Danielle was admitted to Cedars-Sinai hospital with serious complications. The couple had lost an earlier set of twins. This time the doctors were taking no chances. They put Danielle on bedrest. On September 1, 2007, his twin girls were born two months premature. For the next twelve weeks, Morra visited his daughters in the hospital's neonatal intensive care unit, praying they would make it.

Because Danielle was in the hospital with the girls, he didn't want to burden her with the stressful final details of their home. Worried about living in an area known for wildfires, he asked a plumber about putting sprinklers on the roof.

"Great idea," said the plumber. "I could do it for three grand."

It was money Morra didn't have. Building the home cost more than he ever could have imagined. But he wanted to protect his girls, who'd already been through so much. He agreed to the figure and when he told his wife what he'd done, she didn't find it a great idea at all.

Indeed, she was furious.

Fortunately, she quickly forgot about it with the news that the girls were strong enough to go home. Their first dinner as a family was on Thanksgiving. Morra went to bed that evening a grateful man.

At three-thirty the next morning, Danielle was up feeding the twins. She spotted flames on the hillside behind their home and woke up Morra. The house began to shake from the Santa Ana winds as if a locomotive was driving down the hillside. It was a homeowner's—and parent's—worst nightmare.

Morra called 911, and they loaded the girls into the car. He banged on their neighbors' doors, only one of whom he'd met. He'd been so focused on the health of his family and finishing his home that he hadn't made time for introductions. While he knocked on doors, Danielle drove the car down the streets honking her horn. Many of their neighbors might have died if Danielle hadn't been up with two newborn babies.

Later, safely evacuated, Morra and Danielle were watching news coverage to see if their home had made it. Reports were saying over fifty homes in their neighborhood had been destroyed. A reporter walking through the carnage said, "This home survived because of its sprinkler system." The camera panned to their house. The sprinklers on the roof were still pumping water. Morra had remembered to turn them on before he left.

Danielle apologized for ever doubting his decision.

For many of their neighbors, however, the 2007 Corral Fire didn't have a happy ending. At a meeting at Malibu High School, the Corral neighbors gathered to watch a PowerPoint presentation from the fire department, which detailed what a great job the firefighters had done. Many residents were incensed that the firemen were patting themselves on the backs when a quarter of their homes had been lost. The room got loud, and conversations became heated.

The LA County Fire Chief at the time, P. Michael Freeman, seemed to recognize that the department had erred in bragging when so many homeowners were in such pain. He stopped the presentation. "I know we made mistakes," he said to the residents in attendance. "Let's work together to determine what went wrong." He spent the rest of the time taking questions from the crowd and listening to their concerns.

Shortly after the meeting, Freeman created a task force called the Corral Canyon Working Group. Morra was one of seven Corral residents who served on the group. As a result of the disaster, the residents became close and wanted to be better prepared for future fires.

Matt Haines was another resident on the committee. During the '07 fire, Haines used his own water tender (basically a water truck) to drive around the neighborhood putting out fires and saving homes. He received a Citizen of the Year Dolphin Award from *The Malibu Times* in recognition of his efforts.

During their time on the committee, which met once or twice a month, Morra and Haines became friends. Over a couple of beers at Malibu's Barrel restaurant, Haines pitched his idea of creating a volunteer firefighter program for Corral Canyon.

Morra had no desire to be a firefighter. He had a day job in the film business and twin babies at home, but he agreed to use his producer skills to help get the program going. Together they created the Corral Canyon Fire Safety Alliance and raised money to buy two beat-up, twenty-year-old Ford fire engines for $3,500 each.

At the first meeting for the volunteer program, some fifty residents showed up to learn how to pull hoses and handle a nozzle. Many of the volunteers were elderly, but they were determined not to be dependent on the fire department to save their homes in future fires.

One day, Chief Freeman visited Corral Canyon to check on a brush issue the Working Group had identified as a concern. He was with his right-hand man, Daryl Osby, who would be the fire chief in charge during the Woolsey Fire. On the drive up Corral Canyon, Freeman spotted the two fire engines parked on Haines' property.

"What's up with the engines?" Freeman asked with a big smile when he met Morra and Haines at the top of the hill. The men had kept the volunteer program secret since they weren't sure how the real firefighters would take it. Morra was momentarily nonplussed but threw on his producer hat and launched into an explanation of what he and Haines were doing and why they felt it was so necessary. The Calabasas Fire had burned Corral Canyon in 1996. And now there'd been the fire of 2007. It seemed a major fire occurred every ten years and they wanted to be prepared for the next one. With an engine onsite, they'd be able to get to a fire more quickly and put it out before it got out of hand.

"We'd like to start our own volunteer fire department," said Morra, summing up his pitch with a flourish.

Osby appeared taken aback by the suggestion, as if the concept was ludicrous, not to mention dangerous. In the '96 Calabasas Fire, a professional firefighter from Glendale, Bill Jensen, was severely injured in Corral Canyon with burns on seventy percent of his body.

But it was Freeman who'd have the final say. Morra feared Freeman would side with Osby and forbid the whole thing, but the men had built a rapport on the task force. Freeman had implemented a number of Morra's ideas. One was to allow Firehawk helicopters to fly at night, something the task force felt might have stopped the 2007 fire at its ignition point. Another was to bring back Smokey the Bear. As a result, the LA County Fire Department had installed three new Smokey the Bear signs in Malibu warning people about the dangers of throwing cigarettes out the window and reminding them to be more cognizant of their surroundings. (The '07 fire began with an illegal late-night campfire at a cave in the Corral Canyon Hills. A group of drunken men kicked burning wood from the fire outside the cave where strong winds brought the embers into contact with brush. The men involved were sentenced to a year in jail. They were just lucky Danielle was up feeding her twins. Otherwise, the charge might have been murder.)

"I'll do better than that," said Freeman, after hearing Morra out. "Let's create an LA County Call Firefighter program."

"We haven't had a call program in twenty years," said Osby.

From the look on his face, he seemed to want to keep it that way.

Because Freeman was close to retiring, he wasn't worried about doing something that hadn't been done in over two decades. With Freeman's blessing, Morra and Haines began to recruit local residents. Over sixty men and women, old and young, came to the first meeting for the LA County Firefighter Call Program. One of these was Morra's neighbor up the street, Steve Breese. With his glasses and gray-peppered hair, Breese looks like an English professor—or the computer geek he really is. With a master's in computer science from UCLA, he ran a team of systems engineers at an aerospace company.

The local captains at Malibu's Fire Station 71 on Point Dume were put in charge of the program, though they didn't seem happy about training a bunch of middle-aged recruits.

The training started with physical agility tests. The recruits were required to run a seven-minute mile, which most were able to do. It was Southern California after all, and many of the Corral residents ran and hiked regularly in the mountains that surrounded their homes. The next test was a different story. Candidates had to sprint seventy-five feet while dragging 200 feet of fire hose, then make a ninety-degree turn around a barrel and run another twenty-five feet to a taped red square on the ground. Dropping to one knee, the candidate then had to pull the remaining hose into the red square. All in under forty-five seconds.

"If you fail to go around the drum or travel outside the marked path," said the training captain, David Leary, "you fail. If you go outside of the red box, you fail. If you don't keep one knee down at all times you fail. If the nozzle on the end of the hose does not finish in the center of the box, you fail. If you do not complete the test within the allotted time, you fail."

The test seemed designed for all of them to fail, which is why Morra let one of their fittest residents go first. Morra figured he could watch how the guy passed the test.

"That's a fail," Leary said when time ran out before the strongest trainee had finished the course. "You're out of here. There are no second chances fighting a fire."

None of the volunteers had realized that they'd only get one shot. By the end of the day, their group had been cut in half. Somehow, Morra made it through.

Then came the background test.

The group was told to list any bad thing they'd ever done starting in elementary school. If they stole a candy bar, Morra said investigators wanted to know about it. The men were required to list the names of dozens of people throughout their lives—employers, family members, teachers, coaches, friends—all of whom were contacted.

"If you don't tell us something and we find out, you fail."

More people dropped out.

Even tattoos were questioned.

"Why did you get a tattoo? What does it mean?"

There seemed to be no element of their lives the fire department didn't want to know about. As the group edged closer to making it into the training academy, which was the final step, one captain seemed to want to kill the entire program.

With his chiseled jaw, Fire Captain Steve Swiatek looked like Dudley Do-Right but with the attitude of a Marine drill sergeant. He called a meeting with the trainees, a meeting Chief Freeman was not invited to.

"You can't walk into a fire with a latte in your hand," he shouted at Morra and the others, as if that might get them to quit. "Running into a fire isn't like taking a jog with your dog at the beach." He alternately tried to scare and intimidate the men into giving up. Morra wasn't sure why Swiatek was being such a hard ass. The call guys were giving up significant time to train and be of service to their community. Why was there such hostility to the program? But the secret meeting only made the men more determined to move forward.

Next came the medical tests.

Their results had to be perfect. Eyesight needed to be 20/20. A number of the recruits failed. Finally, there were ten men left to enter the academy.

In the summer of 2010, these ten men spent every Saturday and Sunday training under the command of Swiatek, who had started to come around about the group. He witnessed the commitment they showed working full-time jobs, then leaving their families to train every weekend. They crawled into burning buildings. They put out cars on fire. They cleaned latrines. They took written tests on weather conditions and fire behavior. They learned how to drive fire engines, including an old-fashioned stick shift.

Morra struggled to get the pattern right since the lettering on the gear box had been worn away. His difficulties earned him the nickname, "Clutch."

When the ten men graduated and became the first (and only) volunteer firefighters in Malibu, a celebration was held at Duke's Restaurant. Fire Chief Freeman and Captain Swiatek attended, as did Captain David Leary. They'd all become supporters of the men. Malibu fireboats did a water salute. A Firehawk helicopter did a flyover. The men were now officially LA County Call Firefighters. They were issued ID cards and beepers.

All they needed now was a proper fire engine. The old ones they'd purchased were so decrepit they were sold to a photographer, who used them as props in his studio. Morra organized a benefit concert to raise the funds necessary to buy an engine, but also to build a place to store it, something the fire department required. He contacted a friend, famed rock photographer Henry Diltz, who knew members of the band America, known for hits like "Ventura Highway" and "Sister Golden Hair." The band agreed to do the concert for free. Within three weeks, Morra put together the event, which raised over $65,000 for the Corral Canyon Fire Safety Alliance.

With $12,000 of the money, Engine 271 was purchased used from the Orange County Fire Authority. Another $10,000 was spent for the construction of the storage facility on Matt Haines' property. LA County Fire supplied the equipment and communications systems and leased the site (as well as the engine) for one dollar a year.

Soon Morra found himself being paged to go on calls. Originally, the men were supposed to only service Corral Canyon; however, many in the department were impressed with the program and felt it would be beneficial for Engine 271 to be called as needed. It was understood, however, that the engine would never be taken out of Corral Canyon if fire activity was present in the area.

When paged, the men would race to the engine at Haines' house in El Nido. As long as two men were present, the engine was allowed to roll. Most of the initial calls were for medical emergencies, but occasionally their firefighting skills were put to use. Morra and others rappelled down a hillside off Kanan Dume Road to put out a brush fire, the result of a suicidal man driving off the road. As Morra approached the car, he saw the bones of the man inside. When he enrolled in the program to protect his wife and daughters, he had no idea he'd be seeing dead bodies.

As the years went on, there were no fires in Corral Canyon, but the training became more demanding. Instead of working with the firefighters at Fire Station 71 for a few hours every other weekend, the men were expected to go on weekend-long field trips. The additional time commitment forced Morra to resign in 2015.

Still, on the morning of November 9, 2018—even though he was no longer a call firefighter—Morra felt confident that Corral Canyon was prepared, which is why he had no problem with the waiver sheriffs forced him to sign when he stayed behind as his wife and daughters evacuated.

Like most in Malibu, he'd heard the reports of the approaching fire and watched as flames appeared at 10:25 a.m. in the same location as the '07 fire. Unlike that fire, however, this one was moving slowly. The Corral Canyon Fire Safety Alliance had been awarded over $300,000 in grants for brush clearance. They had met with the head of the Forestry Division, J. Lopez, who was an expert in systematic analysis to protect neighborhoods from wildland fire damage. Lopez had advised the alliance on exactly where to remove brush, and the action was now helping to curtail the fire's advance.

Assessing the conditions, Morra called Community Services Liaison Maria Grycan at the command center in Camarillo, asking her to relay to the fire chiefs that the winds were around thirty miles per hour and approximately half the speed of those in 2007. He also called 911 because he wanted the information recorded.

Around noon, low-flying planes began dropping the chemical flame retardant Phos-Chek to create containment lines and prevent the fire from entering the canyon. Two of the planes were smaller, but one was the size of a commercial jet. Right before the jet looked like it was going to crash into the ground, doors on the bottom sprung open, and red retardant covered the hillside. In some cases, the drops covered homes, turning them red.

While Morra appreciated the drops, many of them were off target. Others turned messy with the winds blowing the retardant away from the fire's path. He wasn't concerned, however, as the call firefighters had built relationships with the fire department. The chiefs weren't going to let Corral burn the way it had in 2007.

Steve Breese got a call from one of the volunteer firefighters that Engine 271 had been ordered down to Fire Station 71. Breese figured Engine 271 would pick up one of their local captains, who'd hop on to act as their leader. Engine 271 would then head back up Corral. Breese helped his wife, Kelly, and ten-year-old son load a few last things before they evacuated and headed down to Station 71.

Charlie Case was another call firefighter, but unlike Morra and Breese, who were family men, Case was single. He's in his early sixties, but his lean physique and full head of hair makes him seem as fit, if not fitter, than the younger men. Case's house was the second lowest on the hill, which, in his mind, made it a far safer investment than the other homes in El Nido—and especially those up in the Malibu Bowl area. On the morning of the fire, he drove himself to the top of the canyon. He could see smoke, but he could also tell the fire wouldn't be getting to them anytime soon. That was why he wasn't especially concerned when he received word that Engine 271 had been ordered out of their neighborhood. He figured they would be assigned elsewhere temporarily.

Still, he didn't like it.

When the call firefighters arrived at the fire station with Case at the wheel of Engine 271, they found chaos. Typically, there were five guys at the house, but on the morning of the fire, there were more like twenty. And while there were plenty of firefighters, there seemed to be a shortage of engines.

Case was careful not to get out of his position in the driver's seat. He didn't want to get "snaked" and miss out on his opportunity to fight "the big one." Some discussion was made of adding a couple of professional firefighters to Engine 271, but then an LA County Fire Department battalion chief showed up in a truck with a bunch of firefighters in the back.

"Whose engine is that?" the battalion chief asked, referring to 271.

Case explained that it was the engine for the Corral Canyon community.

"Get your personal gear off of it," the battalion chief said. "We're commandeering it."

Case tried to push back. "This engine isn't funded by LA County. We need to bring it back to our neighborhood."

"That's not going to happen," said the battalion chief. "Get off that engine."

The fire department was set up like the military, something that had been drilled into the men during their training. When an order from a superior was made, it was obeyed. Reluctantly, Case climbed out of the driver's seat.

Inside the station later, Breese lamented the loss of Engine 271, an engine the Corral Community had paid for. They'd spent countless hours training how to use it and now it was gone. Their neighborhood was defenseless again, exactly as it had been in 2007.

"This isn't right," Breese said to the local guy on duty, a firefighter named Danny. Since Station 71 was their parent station, Breese figured he might get some empathy.

"You gonna pull that attitude with me?" Danny asked.

Breese wasn't giving any attitude. He felt like a terrible mistake had been made, one that showed no respect for the sacrifices the men had made. "I don't think our community would appreciate this engine being taken. It's meant to protect the residents of Corral Canyon."

"You think I give a fuck about what your community thinks?" Danny pointed at his badge. "You see what it says here? It says 'firefighter.'"

As if his message wasn't clear enough, the call guys weren't even given a department vehicle to return to their neighborhood. They drove back in Haines' Cadillac. Since they had no sirens or lights to flash, they waved their fireman's hats out the window as Haines crossed onto the wrong side of the gridlocked Pacific Coast Highway. They'd gone from call firefighters to Keystone Cops.

In Corral Canyon, instead of working on the engine as a team, the men were forced to split up. All of their communications equipment was on the engine. Other important safety equipment like deployable shelters were also on the engine. They would have to make do with what they had: garden hoses, fire extinguishers, shovels, dirt.

When Breese returned to his home, he was surprised to find his family still there. Kelly hadn't wanted to leave without being sure he was safe. The news that Engine 271 had been taken seemed to confirm her fears that the family should evacuate together.

Kelly had never embraced the idea of Breese being a call firefighter. She'd agreed with the understanding that the men would be connected to LA County Fire at all times during a wildfire. Now, without their engine, radios, and much of their safety equipment, Kelly was determined for Breese to leave. He tried to have one of the call guys talk to her but she wouldn't budge. They were at a stalemate for hours while Breese laid out what fire hose he could find, hooking it up to hydrants, while keeping an eye on their escape path as the fire crept closer.

At one point, he saw a couple of fire vehicles driving up to the top of the mountain. He walked out to intercept them. LA County Fire Assistant Chief Anthony Williams was in the lead vehicle, followed by a battalion chief from Ventura County. Breese explained he was one of the call guys and that their engine had been commandeered.

"We need engines up here," Breese said.

Williams talked with the battalion chief, who agreed to follow Breese up the hill to look for spots to set engines. Breese took the battalion chief to 71 Alpha, one of the two helicopter landing spots in the area (the other was at Pepperdine University)—71 Alpha is a big, wide-open, relatively safe field.

"Here's a good spot to station some engines," said Breese.

The battalion chief agreed. On the way down the hillside, however, Breese took a short cut zigging and zagging down some of the smaller canyon roads.

The battalion chief flipped on his vehicle's siren, stopped, and got out.

"This area is a no go," he said, apparently spooked by the back roads. "I can't get my engines in here."

Breese drove Engine 271 on these very roads without any problem, and he wasn't a professional firefighter but he couldn't change the chief's mind.

"It doesn't matter what you say," the chief said. "I'm done."

At their house, Kelly still refused to leave without him.

"You are coming with me," she said, "or we are staying and we will all die together."

Kelly knew Breese would never let their young son stay. Finally, he agreed to leave.

Down the street, Morra was prepping nearby houses, utilizing his academy training. Because the Corral neighborhood used propane for cooking, he went to every home and shut off their gas. He turned on the sprinklers on his roof and began to wet the decks of his home and his neighbor's house. By 3:00 p.m., he began to worry, however, as there were no engines. The winds were strong, but the fire was still manageable. He drove down Corral Canyon to search for engines. On PCH, he ran into an LA County battalion chief and explained his past as one of the call firefighters. The chief said he'd drive his Suburban up to assess the situation. Morra waited on PCH with some other neighbors.

"You're looking good for now," the chief told Morra when he returned after taking a look. "But I'm going to get some engines in here."

Later, five engines from Oxnard and Ventura County drove into the Malibu Bowl section of Corral. Morra's home was on the front line of where the fire would hit first, but when he returned to his house, the engines were parked on the opposite side of the bowl—far from where the fire would hit. He tried to explain that the men were parked in the wrong spot, thinking it must be an accident.

"We've had no communications with LA County Fire," one of the captains said. "We're not doing anything without orders."

Mora was stunned. They surely had been told to come into Corral to protect homes. But when the captain kept repeating his refrain, it became clear they weren't going to do anything. Just after 5:00 p.m., over seven hours after flames had first become visible, the fire exploded in the Malibu Bowl area. Morra raced down to PCH and spotted another five or six engines lined up near the 76 gas station. He and another resident, Susie Duff, pleaded for the engines to head up Corral. Over and over, the response was "we're waiting for orders."

One battalion chief took exception when he felt Morra had gone too far while begging for help.

"Don't you ever point a finger in my face," the chief screamed.

Morra told me he feared the chief was going to punch him in the face. "Please, we need structure protection," he pleaded yet again, keeping his fingers to himself.

"Did you not hear what I said? It's too late for the upper bowl."

But there were no homes on fire yet in the upper bowl area. Instead, the chief took his engines toward the El Nido area below Morra's home.

On the way back up Corral Canyon, Morra encountered the two engines from Oxnard. They were sitting on the side of the road outside of El Nido, which they refused to enter.

The engines stayed parked on Corral until approximately midnight when they took off, apparently for Pepperdine, where flames were threatening the students who hadn't evacuated as part of Pepperdine's shelter-in-place policy.

Around the time the engines left, the residents who stayed lost hydrant water. Dozens of homes started to burn. If it weren't for the efforts of the call firefighters, fighting with hand tools and boots, many more homes would've been lost. In the El Nido neighborhood, the call firefighters and others saved all but one home. In the Malibu Bowl area, over twenty homes were lost.

Even though their homes survived, Morra and Breese took these losses personally. No neighborhood had been better prepared. No community had forged stronger relationships with the fire department. Yet, they'd been abandoned. Breese felt he'd let down the call firefighters by evacuating and broke down in tears when he tried to talk about it. He felt humiliated, not by his wife forcing him to leave, but by the way the fire department had treated them. Both men were positive that if Engine 271 hadn't been commandeered, the presence of the engine in the Malibu Bowl would've made other engines feel confident enough to stay and defend homes. Morra wondered why firefighters had come to the area at all. By his count, approximately ten engines sat and did nothing in Corral, a colossal waste of resources, as well as a complete betrayal of everything he'd spent eleven years working on.

Engine 271 didn't get back to its rightful owners until Monday, three days after the fire started. The engine wasn't even returned to Station 71. Instead, it was dumped in the parking lot of Zuma Beach. The call firefighters had no idea how long it was sitting there or whether homes could've been saved in Corral Canyon if they'd been given a heads-up where it was. By the time they picked it up, the Woolsey Fire was essentially out.

Part of the reason the engine had been taken?

To save an LA County fire station.

Kevin Webb wearing the uniform of locals who fought the fire: thick coat, goggles, gloves, jeans, and head protection. He is missing a mask and a good pair of boots.

PHOTO BERL DAHLSTROM

3

LAST OF THE RAMBO FIREFIGHTERS

Wearing an LA County Fire T-shirt, Berl Dahlstrom looks like the firefighter he was for thirty-five years. He's in his mid-eighties now, though, and his mustache is white. Berl became a firefighter in 1957 and worked his way up from engineer to fire captain to battalion chief. He moved to Calpine Drive in the Malibu Park neighborhood in the '70s when no one wanted to live in Malibu. The commute was too far to get to places like Beverly Hills or West Hollywood where Berl served before retiring in 1992. Aside from a few famous actors and music legends who didn't keep consistent hours—or have a regular commute—Malibu was filled with blue collar types like Berl. The ocean and clean air were part of the draw but mainly back then Malibu was cheap. The western half was practically uninhabited and considered "the sticks" enabling teachers, sheriffs, and firefighters to buy homes they couldn't have afforded anywhere else.

Early the Friday morning of the fire, Berl had a visitor at his home, Anthony Williams, one of the assistant chiefs of the LA County Fire Department. The fire department has lots of "chiefs," though they aren't all at the same level. Daryl Osby is the main chief and the head of the department. But Osby has a couple of chief deputies, along with seven or eight deputy chiefs. If that isn't confusing enough, there are also assistant chiefs who are higher than battalion chiefs, who in turn are higher than fire captains. When I interviewed Berl, he explained the hierarchy to me and still I was confused by it. He said so were some in the fire department.

In his heyday, Berl had as many as twelve fire captains reporting to him. He also trained many of the leaders who would eventually be in charge during the Woolsey Fire, including Deputy Chief Vince Pena, one of the department's top commanders. Because of Berl's reputation, history, and age, Assistant Chief Williams had come to the Dahlstrom home to ask Berl and his wife, Pat, to evacuate.

"You've got three hours until the fire gets here," Williams said.

"I'm not leaving," said Berl.

"I wish you would. This one is going to be bad." Williams explained that his request for an additional seventy engines had been denied since extra resources were being sent to northern California to fight the Camp Fire in Paradise, which started the day before the Woolsey Fire.

Berl shook his head. "I've got Kevin to help me."

Kevin Webb is Berl's stepson and a physical fitness buff. Most mornings Kevin could be found running on the soft sand at Zuma Beach before dawn. His daily run was ten miles. Later in the day he'd hop in the Malibu High School pool, where he worked as a lifeguard, and swim for an hour. Kevin grew up in Malibu, and though not a firefighter, he'd fought several fires. His nickname was Sparky, though that came more as a result of how much weed he'd smoked in the late '70s.

"Don't worry about us," Berl said. "Kevin and I will make do."

After Williams left, Kevin, Berl, and Pat went into prep mode. They began spacing trash cans out on their property, filling them with water just as Millie Decker had done as a young girl in Malibu in the early 1900s. In lieu of the gunnysacks she used, however, they wet towels and hung them on the sides of the cans to whip out spot fires. They moved anything that might burn away from the house or put it inside. Berl had seen many homes destroyed because of lawn furniture, which caught fire and led to the house burning. Wood piles were another fuel source people often didn't consider though, in his mind, the worst thing you could do was plant fuel beside your house in the form of flammable trees.

Berl had good brush clearance on his property, known as "defensible space" in firefighting lingo. He believed a couple of prepared and able-bodied people could save a home if it had good clearance. He felt folks who bought a home in a fire-prone area like Malibu should have some rudimentary knowledge of what to do when the inevitable happened. They should have the right clothing—masks, boots, gloves, goggles, and a thick coat—as well as a week's worth of food and water. They should expect they'll be on their own. But, over the years, those who'd moved to Malibu were city folk or suburbanites. The new neighbors didn't seek out the advice of long-time locals like Berl. When the evacuation call came they fled, sure that firefighters would save their homes.

So when the wall of flames rose over Horizon Drive, the vast majority of residents were already gone. The winds were whipping down Zuma Canyon, pushing the fire quickly into the neighborhood. Houses immediately started to catch. Because so few people stayed, no one was there to stop the domino effect. Soon Malibu Park was burning down.

Berl and his wife, Pat, along with Kevin went into their home when the initial firestorm hit. He knew it would pass quickly and that the safest place to be then was inside. Homes didn't just spontaneously combust. They took time to burn down. The rumbling wind sounded like a crashing waterfall as the storm passed over them. The house shook like it might be ripped from its foundation—or come apart in pieces.

When the fury subsided, the family sprang into action. They circled the perimeter of the property, putting out the many embers they found. For bigger fires, Kevin, Berl, or Pat would whap a wet towel onto them, dousing the fire with water and depriving it of oxygen. Unfortunately, a hedge on a neighboring property caught fire. Driven by the strong winds, thousands of embers flew directly toward the Dahlstrom home. They tried repeatedly to put the hedge out, but the fire quickly grew beyond control. They were in danger of losing their home because of someone else's brush. Right when the fire was at its worst, a Firehawk helicopter emerged from the clouds of black smoke covering the neighborhood. The pilots were waving at Berl like they knew him, which they did. The Firehawk maneuvered over the hedge and let rip with a water drop that instantly put the fire out.

It was the only helicopter Berl would see in Malibu Park. He saw no firefighters. But between three people, two in their mid-eighties, they were able to save their house, as well as a number of other nearby homes. Another neighbor, Paul Phillipson, simply used his feet, stomping out flames wherever he saw them. His home survived, too, though it suffered heavy damage when the winds imploded his doors and windows. Not one of these residents was under fifty. Most were far older. Yet they (and others) saved their homes without a single injury. The first fire engine Berl spotted in the neighborhood was late Saturday afternoon, well over twenty-four hours after the fire had entered Malibu Park. By then, he had heard rumors of firefighters refusing to fight the fire. To Berl, the idea was unfathomable.

"We saw a fire. We fought the fire," he said about his days as a battalion chief. He bemoaned the new, risk-averse attitude the young people seemed to come into the department with. When I asked Berl why firefighters hadn't engaged, he shook his head.

"They should get off their asses and get to work," he said, "instead of cowering inside their engines." I suggested that many of the firefighters didn't know the areas within Malibu since they had come from other jurisdictions but to him this was no excuse.

"They needed to do what they needed to do."

Many residents spotted fire engines sitting idly by the side of the road while the fire raged. Some in the fire department claimed this was just men taking breaks.

"There's never a break when fighting a fire," Berl told me.

Furthermore, he wondered why Zuma Beach had been used as a staging area when Malibu High School was available. The school was located right in the middle of the Malibu Park neighborhood and contained a massive pool for firefighters to use as a water source. Berl believed homes could have been saved if firefighters had been based at the school. Instead, in a neighborhood of 275 homes, approximately 180 had been lost.

While Berl didn't see any firefighters on the ground in Malibu Park, there were a few. One LA County Fire captain, who asked to remain anonymous because of the backlash he feared, came upon an engine parked on the side of the road doing nothing. I'll call him "Rambo."

"You need to get to work," Rambo told the engine's captain.

"Who the hell are you?" the man asked.

"It doesn't matter who I am. I need you to engage."

"Well, I don't feel comfortable."

Rambo pointed at a nearby cluster of homes, only one of which was burning. "You can save those homes."

"Well—"

"Stop 'well'-ing me and get to work. Sitting here isn't going to put it out. Back your engine in if you're so worried about getting caught. Otherwise, why don't you just go home?"

Rambo didn't want to waste any more time trying to convince the captain and headed toward his engine. But as he pulled away, he saw the other engine backing up toward the homes.

Rambo "tuned up" other firefighters that day.

"Get out there," he'd holler at those sitting around. "You can protect homes."

Some listened, some didn't. At the very least, he felt captains should have been getting out of their engines to assess the situation. If you didn't even assess, you simply weren't doing your job.

One firefighter that Rambo would have been proud to serve with was Captain Edward Smith. Ed lived in the city of Ventura and had been a firefighter for twenty-three years. He spent seven years running firefighting inmate crews, which often didn't have water and relied on tools like shovels (and feet) to put fires out.

When he arrived at Fire Station 73 in Newhall that Friday morning, the station's engine was already gone. A call came in that two firefighters were needed to replace others who'd been on initial action for the Woolsey Fire. Firefighters on initial action stayed on duty until they were replaced—or the fire went out. The men they were replacing had been working since the prior afternoon.

"I'll do it," said Ed. He grabbed a probationary firefighter, Blake Wein, who'd only been on the job three months. They made their way to Malibu in Patrol 73, a smaller firefighting vehicle with 250 gallons of water, half the amount engines carried. Patrol 65 with Captain Jon Obringer and Jon Galiher followed behind them. When Ed arrived in Malibu's Trancas Canyon area, other rigs were already there. Ed saw a column of black smoke coming from an area near the Malibu High School and headed in that direction.

The roads into the Malibu Park neighborhood were nearly impassable. Downed power poles and power lines covered the streets. A normal-sized engine wouldn't have made it through, but their smaller patrols were able to squeeze around the debris. Homes were burning all around them but the hydrants in the neighborhood were dry. If there'd been water, Ed could've blasted a bunch of the homes to see if any were salvageable.

Instead, they drove by them.

The men came upon a little blue house sandwiched between two homes on fire. Flames shot high into the air from the gas line of one of the homes. Ed got out and shut off the line, studying the home to see if he could save it. The brush clearance was pretty good. If the homeowner had planted flammable trees or vegetation near the home, Ed would've walked away. Spending his water on such a home would have been a waste. He told Blake, "We're going to save this one."

Wearing gloves, the men climbed onto the roof and cleared leaves from the gutters, something the homeowner had neglected to do. Flames from the house next door were sending embers into the wood siding of the blue house. The winds kept pushing at those embers, fanning them larger and pushing them deeper into the wood. Because of his time with the inmate crews, Ed was used to conserving water when fighting a wildfire. For hours, he and the other firefighters spritzed small amounts of water onto the home, while waiting for the adjacent home to finish burning.

But he didn't have enough water to put the embers out, which were glowing red and now embedded in a section of the home's siding. No matter what he did, he couldn't get them out. He was going to lose the home, which meant he'd wasted his water. He didn't have enough left to save any others.

"Get the chainsaw," he yelled to Blake.

Blake ran to the patrol vehicle and grabbed the chainsaw. Ed cut out a huge section of the smoldering siding then kept spritzing what remained to keep more wind-driven embers from burrowing into the wood. Ed and the other men spent three hours at the house until they were sure it was safe. One missed ember could burn down a house. Ed was not going to let that happen. When they finally left, the little blue house was one of the only homes on the street to survive.

Later, Ed and Blake refilled their patrol and saved other houses, including the home of Julia Roberts' mother. At one point, they even had a civilian work one of their hoses. Together with Blake, the three of them saved a cluster of homes. The Woolsey Fire was an "all hands on deck" situation. There were so many houses on fire, Ed would just pick one. He certainly didn't wait for orders since he knew resources were stretched thin.

During the 2017 Thomas Fire, Ed had been listening when the Ventura County dispatcher called for one hundred engines and received fewer than ten so he wasn't expecting any more help. Huge, fast moving fires were the new "abnormal." Firefighters were seeing speed rates they'd never seen before. Ed knew there was no stopping a wind-driven fire once it crossed the 101 Freeway, but that didn't mean he was giving up—or idly sitting by.

Having so many firefighters refusing to engage not only made his job harder that day, it brought shame to the department—and to the profession. For every ten good things firefighters did during the Woolsey Fire, it was the one bad thing that people would remember.

In the case of my neighbor in the little blue house, though, only love and gratitude existed for firefighters like Ed Smith.

Valerie's untouched Gypsy Wagon and garden.

PHOTO VALERIE SKLARLEVSKY

4

LICENSE TO KILL

Valerie Sklarevsky lived on Point Dume in Malibu in a 200-year-old English covered wagon with no heat, electricity, or running water. I met Valerie when she signed up for the creative writing class I taught for the city of Malibu. I might have gone easier on her had I known Bob Dylan wrote a song about her.

The covered wagon had been shipped to Hollywood for the movie *Doctor Doolittle* starring Rex Harrison. After filming, the wagon was offered to anyone willing to haul it away. A cardiologist, Alan Weiss, and his wife, Donna, brought it to their property as they thought their young daughters would like to play in the wagon.

Valerie had other ideas.

She'd moved to Malibu from the Baltimore area in the early '80s to escape the radiation she feared from the nuclear accident at Three Mile Island, an event which was to shape her life—and her career as an activist. Valerie's mantra was to live simply so that others might simply live.

She was living in a nearby teepee when she spotted the ocean view wagon.

I want to live in a Gypsy wagon, she thought, entranced.

That night, she slept under a large pine tree on the property and prayed to be able to live there. In the morning, she knocked on the door of the main house.

"I just need a quiet place," she said. "Could I rent your wagon?"

The owners agreed for $40 per month along with some minor caretaking duties. In 1981, she moved in and left an "I'm your new neighbor" note for her next door neighbor, who turned out to be Bob Dylan. To her surprise, he hopped over the chain link fence that separated their properties to say hi. Perhaps he'd spotted the attractive thirty-year-old blonde naked and washing herself using a solar shower she'd attached to the pine tree. This was the beginning of a nearly forty-year friendship. Valerie didn't even have doors on the wagon. She used blankets to keep the heat in and the rain out, until Bob had doors brought over one day.

Living in such a minimal space with such minimal needs allowed her to focus her energies on her true calling—protesting war and protecting the environment, especially as it related to nuclear weapons and nuclear power. Her activism took off in Malibu resulting in her being arrested fifty-four times. Bob immortalized her efforts in the song "License to Kill" for his *Infidels* album.

> Man thinks 'cause he rules the earth he can do with it as he please
> And if things don't change soon, he will
>
> But there's a woman on my block
> Sitting there in a cold chill
> She say who gonna take away his license to kill?

In 1982, Valerie hiked with singer Jackson Browne and others onto the grounds of the Diablo Canyon Nuclear Power Plant in the middle of the night to show that the facility was poorly protected. The guards couldn't believe the activists had gotten past them and so close to the plant.

"We're just kids. What if we were terrorists?" she asked with her thick Baltimore accent as they arrested her.

In 1986, Valerie protested at the site of another nuclear power plant—the Santa Susana Field Laboratory in the hills of Simi Valley. In 1959, a partial nuclear meltdown occurred there, which was kept secret from the public for twenty years. Valerie had friends who'd been protesting, but one woman, Lisa Apper, felt they weren't getting enough attention. The flyers the activists tried to hand out to employees were routinely taken and destroyed by security. Some of the employees seemed interested since many of them were likely in the dark about the dangers of working at the facility, but security kept blocking the activists from engaging with the staff. Valerie wanted to do something dramatic to get a personal encounter with management, which was impossible to do from the sidewalk. She and Lisa decided to risk arrest. They chose the date of their action to attract the attention of the press: August 6, the anniversary of the Hiroshima atomic bomb.

In a coordinated move, a group of activists went to one end of the building while Valerie and Lisa slipped away. The two women walked inside the other end, pretending they worked there, handing out flyers to anyone they met. They'd made it to the cafeteria when a security guard recognized Lisa as one of the activists.

"Stop," he shouted, and the women halted. "You need to leave right now."

But the women didn't obey. Valerie and Lisa calmly waited for the police to arrive and arrest them. Multiple newspapers ran her story the next day. Valerie kept the police report, which lists the only thing she had in her possession: one remaining flyer.

Professor Dan Hirsch knew more about the ignition point of the Woolsey Fire—the Santa Susana Field Laboratory (SSFL) in Simi Valley—than anyone in the world. Located less than thirty miles from Malibu, the nearly 3,000-acre site had been used since the late '40s for the development of rocket engines. In the '50s, Atomics International began to use the SSFL for the development of nuclear reactors. In 1979, Hirsch and his UCLA students discovered there'd been a secret nuclear meltdown on the site in 1959, which released hundreds of times more radionuclides than the meltdown at Three Mile Island. The

Atomics International reactor didn't even have a containment dome and wasn't shut down until thirteen days *after* the first signs of trouble. Radioactive materials were intentionally vented into the atmosphere to prevent the reactor from exploding, releasing nuclear radiation into the skies above Greater Los Angeles.

Professor Hirsch leads the Committee to Bridge the Gap, a nonprofit nuclear policy organization that focuses on issues of nuclear safety, waste disposal, proliferation, and disarmament. He is also the director of the Program on Environmental and Nuclear Policy at the University of California, Santa Cruz, and a former director of the Adlai Stevenson Program on Nuclear Policy.

When I called him to discuss the ramifications of a wildfire starting on the SSFL site, Hirsch spoke rapidly, bandying about words like cesium-139, strontium-90, and plutonium-239, apparently the deadliest substance on earth. Not only had there been a partial meltdown in 1959, there were three smaller accidents at other reactors on the site. Employees were given Bactine to clean off the walls. They used Kotex pads for the floors since they were so absorbent, and were ordered to tell no one, including their spouses.

Because the SSFL had once been owned by Rocketdyne, a rocket and engine design company, the site had also seen over 30,000 rocket engine tests. Hirsch called SSFL "the most contaminated site in the United States," and described a witch's brew of over one hundred different toxins, including PCBs, mercury, tritium, perchlorate, as well as cesium-139, strontium-90, and plutonium-239. A UCLA study released in 1997 estimated that between 300 and 1800 people developed cancer and died as a result of the 1959 meltdown. Those numbers didn't include cancers from the other nuclear accidents or the 30,000 engine tests.

What I wanted to know was if—or how many—of those toxins reached Malibu on the day of the Woolsey Fire driven by the relentless seventy mile an hour Santa Ana winds. Specifically, was the water in my son's high school pool safe? Davis is on the swim team and swims in that water daily. My wife had fought the Santa Monica Malibu Unified School District to change the water after the fire, but they told her they couldn't find anyone willing to take the pool water. Instead, they "cleaned" it.

"What about the water in the Malibu pool?" I asked Hirsch. "Is it safe from contaminants? They did reverse osmosis on it."

"Reverse osmosis is pretty good," Hirsch said.

I breathed a sigh of relief and heard what sounded like another phone ringing.

"Though it doesn't remove tritium," he added.

Before I could ask what that might do to a teenage boy, he excused himself to take the other call. While he did, I googled the chemical and read that tritium can be inhaled, ingested, or absorbed through the skin, two of which could occur in a pool. I glanced at another article that said the public was only now becoming aware of the magnitude of tritium's hazards. Studies indicated that tritium could cause cancer, genetic defects, developmental abnormalities, and reproductive effects. Though I swam in the pool too, I was most concerned for my son.

When he came back on the line, he said, "I don't think you need to panic about the pool. The smoke you breathed from the fire was probably worse."

I think he meant this as good news, but I wasn't comforted since I'd also made my son stay to fight the fire. I didn't want to seem unprofessional asking more questions about what I'd done to my kid and instead asked what his thoughts were when he first heard about the Woolsey Fire.

"It should have been put out right away," he said. "The fire was very small."

Southern California Edison had an outage with a circuit located on the SSFL site at 2:22 p.m. Two minutes later, flames were sighted in Woolsey Canyon near that location. Stu Mundel, an LA area reporter for Sky9, a local television station, was overhead in a helicopter and took a picture just after the fire broke out, which Hirsch saw on Twitter.

But because Boeing, which now owned the abandoned SSFL site, had dismantled much of the complex's fire suppression system, they'd eliminated their ability to fight fires, even small ones. Boeing had zero firefighters and supplied limited access to water. LA County Deputy Fire Chief Vince Pena said the moment to stop the Woolsey Fire was on the SSFL site.

Using Google Earth, Hirsch was able to estimate that the fire had started less than 1,000 feet from the site of the '59 meltdown, which meant that toxic radioactive materials in the soil and in the burned vegetation were being blown by the winds and landing elsewhere. After the fire, my neighbor showed me a melted lawnmower on his property. When I didn't seem especially impressed, he said, "You don't get it. It's not my lawnmower."

The winds had blown it down from someone else's house.

Hirsch said the entire region was "dusted with contaminants." One estimate said the fire released over 40,000 tons of ash loaded with radiation and chemicals.

It was a situation that never should have occurred—even if there was a fire—since the US Department of Energy had committed in 2010 to clean up the site by 2017. Boeing had signed a similar order in 2007. A $40 million EPA study in 2012 showed astronomical levels of radiation in the area. Strontium-90 tested 284 times normal. Cesium-137 was 9,328 times normal. Plutonium-239 was 92 times normal *twenty-four feet below the soil surface.*

Yet, on the day of the Woolsey Fire, the cleanup hadn't been started.

Hirsch told me Boeing had hired regulators and lobbyists who were former aides to California Governor Jerry Brown in an attempt to "run out the clock" on their commitments. Indeed, only weeks after the fire, the Trump administration's DOE announced plans to walk away from their agreements and leave ninety-eight percent of the contaminants where they are.

Even if no one ever lived on the site again, the contaminants can still travel. The SSFL site sits high atop a hill, which makes the migration of toxins easier. Following the Woolsey Fire, an El Niño weather pattern brought heavy rains, likely further spreading the toxins, which existed in far greater concentrations than legally allowed.

Hirsch worried that the surrounding areas, which included a cattle farm, would now also be contaminated. The Simi Valley area still is host to lots of agriculture. The SSFL site was originally a farm. Who would want to drink the milk or eat the meat of animals grazing on land packed with radioactive and chemical poisons? Would the public even be told their milk or meat came from the area around the SSFL? While Hirsch admitted the SSFL was not Chernobyl or Fukushima, that didn't mean people wouldn't get sick.

Or that people wouldn't die.

Studies have shown those closest to the SSFL site were at the greatest risk, but with the fire, the winds, and the rain, "close" is a relative term. Deputy Fire Chief Vince Pena said embers from a eucalyptus tree can travel twenty-five miles. Malibu is about that distance from the SSFL. How far can one speck of radioactive material go?

With the recent rains, vegetation was already starting to grow at the site. Without remediation, the brush would simply wait for another fire to again spread its poisons. With no plan in place for a cleanup, a proposal was made for something else on the SSFL site.

An open space park.

It already has a name, unofficial though it may be.

The "Glow in the Dark" park.

When Valerie heard that the Woolsey Fire had originated on the grounds of the SSFL, her worst lifelong fears were realized. Despite her efforts, which included two nights in jail, she knew the site had never been cleaned up.

Oh my God, those poisons are coming to Malibu, she thought.

Ten hours after the fire started, authorities claimed no danger to the public existed, despite the fact they hadn't had time for any testing, let alone obtaining the results. Valerie believed it was cheaper for Boeing to pay off regulators and wait for activists like her to die off, rather than to properly dispose of radioactive materials. Indeed, approximately two months *before* the fire, the California Department of Toxic Substances Control was supposed to have released a "decision document," which would have delineated its cleanup plan for the site. Instead, they said there was no anticipated date for the document, let alone for the work to begin, despite the fact that they'd signed binding agreements to clean up the contamination.

Now those toxins were being driven by Santa Ana winds and a fire burning contaminated vegetation and brush, potentially sending plutonium-239 all the way to the beach. Valerie worried about the children of Malibu, though she wished they'd spend more time keeping up with their environment rather than keeping up with the Kardashians since no safe amount existed for any of these materials. (In an odd twist, Kim Kardashian and her sister, Kourtney, turned out at an event in July 2019 to commemorate the sixtieth anniversary of the nuclear accident at the SSFL—and to call for action to clean up the contaminated site. Like most in the area, they'd had no idea of the toxins in their backyards.)

The Friday of the fire, Bob Dylan's barking mastiffs woke Valerie at 2:00 a.m. She could smell smoke. A few hours later, she walked the dog of Rick Rubin, Grammy award winning producer of artists like the Red Hot Chili Peppers and the Dixie Chicks. Valerie had been walking Rubin's dog for ten years, one of her many part-time jobs. She wasn't going to let a fire stop her, though she noticed two columns of smoke over the mountains. She said they resembled devil's horns.

And they were coming straight toward Malibu.

Valerie hurried back to the Gypsy Wagon and packed a small suitcase, along with her most important possession: her four large Tupperware containers of paperwork related to her years of activism.

Valerie drove around Point Dume and saw large amounts of smoke, but most of the neighbors she spoke with didn't seem concerned. Over and over she heard, "Point Dume has never burned." She tried to evacuate down the Pacific Coast Highway, but the road was gridlocked. Finally, she convinced herself her neighbors were right and headed back to the safety of Point Dume. She was napping in the Gypsy Wagon when her neighbor, Jeff Stockwell, woke her.

"The fire's on Point Dume," he shouted.

She rushed into her car and headed down Dume Drive as flaming embers "the size of fists" hurtled though the air, pounding against the windows and the doors. Sheriffs were yelling, "Get out! Get out! Go south to Santa Monica."

Valerie had never felt such fear before. Whenever she was about to protest, she told herself, "Step into your fear." Even being arrested wasn't scary. Valerie found it exhilarating.

"That's why I did it so many times," she said, referring to her fifty-four arrests.

But the Woolsey Fire was different. All her activism hadn't affected her the way the fire did. She felt a sense of doom, as if the world was ending. She evacuated to her niece's home in the Palisades.

The next morning, Jeff texted that in her neighborhood of multimillion-dollar estates, just Bob Dylan's house had survived. The only other exception: the Gypsy Wagon.

But she wasn't out of the woods yet, for fires were still consuming homes, especially on Point Dume. The winds were scheduled to pick up as well, stirring embers and blowing them onto homes. A few more anxious days went by. Valerie texted her friend Peggy Idema, the mother of Anthony Kiedis, the lead singer of the Red Hot Chili Peppers, to find out if her wagon was still there. Peggy sent Anthony over and what he found shocked them all. The entire hillside was black, but both the Gypsy Wagon and Valerie's garden had survived. The rest looked like a scorched moonscape. Anthony told his mother he thought Valerie must have some powerful guardians watching over her.

Valerie's elation was short lived. Over fifty of her friends had lost their homes. Bob Dylan sent over one of his workers to replace the tarp on the top of the Gypsy Wagon, which had melted during the fire but somehow didn't burn it down.

Valerie went to stay in Camarillo with the daughter of her landlord, but the family didn't seem so happy about her good news.

"Why did your place survive and our house didn't?" one daughter asked.

"Looks like you're homeless now too," said another.

Valerie hadn't even been back yet. Her belongings were still in the wagon, but because the family's main home was gone, they were putting the property up for sale. Asking price? $8 million.

The fire didn't burn the Gypsy Wagon, but it took Valerie's home nonetheless.

Afterwards, there were many stories like this. People living in guest houses or basement apartments or other structures (like Valerie's Gypsy Wagon) were kicked out. Even if their place hadn't burned, the main home was often gone or damaged. Owners needed to move into their other units, forcing renters onto the streets. The count of lost homes, which was close to 1,000, didn't include unpermitted structures like Valerie's wagon. The true number of places lost to the fire, of lives upended, was likely double. Valerie also lost her jobs, as did countless others. Many of the rich and famous, who often had multiple homes, jetted to locations that weren't federal disaster areas. This left their staff and service providers without work.

Valerie decided to move to the Bahamas to live with her brother. Since only Bahamians could work there, she was officially retired. I hope the Bahamians have their environmental act together. Otherwise, there would be arrest number fifty-five.

Oh, and high on a hill overlooking the ocean sits a 200-year-old English covered wagon with one hell of a history. Fire-resistant too.

All you have to do is haul it away.

This is a mural of Valerie's fifty-four arrests.
Note actor/activist Martin Sheen in the lower right corner.
PHOTO VALERIE SKLARLEVSKY

The Gonzalez home before the fire.

PHOTO DAVE TEEL

5

A STUDENT'S LOSS

Nina Gonzalez was in her senior year at Malibu High when the Woolsey fire struck. She was one of the stars of the school's competitive theatre program. Because of Malibu's longstanding connection to Hollywood, many of the theatre kids are the children (or grandchildren) of famous movie stars or major film producers. Getting a lead role in a Malibu High School show means beating out the offspring of Oscar winners and Tony award nominees. Productions have access to Hollywood costume and prop shops. Famous composers work with the school band in the orchestra pit. No expense is spared to create productions that rival the Broadway originals.

Or at least the touring company.

I first spotted Nina in a production of *James and the Giant Peach.* My son had a small part while Nina played one of the leads. With her dark hair and expressive eyes, she reminded me of Winona Ryder in *Beetlejuice.* With all due respect to my son's compelling delivery of his one line, Nina Gonzalez was the best actor in that show. But unlike many of the others in the cast who came from families with a background in show business, Nina has no leg up. Her mother, Jennifer, teaches English at the high school. Her father, John, is a dentist. Typical of the people who lost homes in the Woolsey Fire, they were not rich or famous. In fact, Jennifer and John had built their log cabin home in 1996 *by themselves.*

The homesteaders who settled in the area in the late 1800s would have been proud.

Built on stilts and resembling a treehouse, the Gonzalez home was off Kanan Dume Road and up Latigo Canyon in an area particularly vulnerable to wildfires. Having lived her entire life in the house, Nina had seen more than a few fires get close. The morning of November 9, her mother woke her at 3:00 a.m. to evacuate.

"You need to go," Jennifer told Nina and a friend who was sleeping over. "Don't worry, everything's going to be fine. The house will still be here when you get back."

Nina took only a few things: a suitcase she hadn't unpacked from a trip to visit NYU's Tisch School of Dramatic Arts (one of the premier acting schools in the country), a few original drawings she'd made, and a hand-painted poster from her favorite movie, *Amelie.*

Jennifer and John were determined to save the home they'd built. They had a 5,000-gallon water tank, a fire pump, and 450 feet of fire hose. They tested the pump every year. John was prepared to fight, though Jennifer promised she would leave if it got bad.

"It's just stuff," Jennifer told Nina. "My daughter needs a mother."

To Nina's father, however, the home was more than stuff. He was a sculpture artist and a pilot. He'd combined his two hobbies and built his own four-seat propeller airplane, which he kept in a hangar. But in his basement, he had dozens of airplane models that he'd made himself. Many of them were gliders. Also, John's father had died a month earlier, so all of his dad's possessions were in the house: jewelry, clothes, sentimental items like a fishing rod.

A few hours after the girls left, Jennifer heard the fire had jumped the freeway. She knew there would be no support from firefighters since their home was too far up the canyon. They were on their own, but she felt prepared. They planned to let the initial firestorm go through and then use the pump to put out embers and spot fires. The home was constructed with ten-inch diameter

Douglas Fir logs. While they were wood, they were so thick that they would take a while to catch fire. This would give the couple time.

At 6:30 a.m., Jennifer and John drove to the lookout at the top of the Castro Peak Motorway and saw flames in the distance, confirming their worst fears.

They hurried home to set up the pump and the hoses. They tested it, just to be safe, and the pump worked great, shooting water high into the sky.

At 7:30 a.m., it was still outside—as still as it could possibly be. Then Jennifer heard a "rumbling."

It was the roar of brush being consumed by the flames.

As the fire came closer, it sounded like a freight train. Suddenly, flames were coming over the ridge behind their backyard.

"You need to take the dogs and go," John yelled through his respirator mask. "I've got this. I've been preparing my whole life for this."

She didn't want to leave without him, but she couldn't talk him out of staying. Finally, Jennifer left the neighborhood and drove down the canyon. When she turned onto Kanan Dume Road to head toward the ocean, she passed the Rosenthal Winery. It was on fire. Flames had been *behind* her home minutes earlier, now they were *ahead* of her. Above her, a black line of smoke met the blue of the sky but the black was taking over. She sped down the road to not get trapped by the flames—and to catch what was left of the blue.

Jennifer caught up with Nina at a friend's home in the Malibu West neighborhood across from Zuma Beach where they'd agreed to rendezvous. "I think most of our neighborhood is gone," Jennifer said. "But if anyone can stop the fire, it'll be your dad."

By then, flames had reached Malibu West too.

They helped the family pack their stuff, which was surreal since Nina had taken so few things of her own. Each item she loaded reminded her of what she'd left behind. They evacuated again, this time across the PCH to the parking lot at Zuma Beach. There they found the beach divided almost exactly in half. The eastern side was still normal with blue skies, kids playing ball, even a girl out surfing. The western side was covered in a cloud of billowing, black smoke, growing larger with each second.

"Watching Malibu burn and not being able to do a thing about it was the hardest part," Jennifer told me. "The scene was horrifying, mesmerizing, and occasionally beautiful. Seeing large animals like alpacas and llamas walking on the sand was breathtaking, as if a zoo had burned down."

Around 11:00 a.m., Jennifer spotted John sitting on one of the sand dunes. Though it was a huge relief to find him, she knew right away their home was gone.

"The pump froze," he said. "I couldn't get it to work."

"I'm so glad you left," said Jennifer. "If it looks this bad at the beach, I can't imagine what it was like up in the canyon."

Nina ran into friends who hoped the school *would* burn down. The high school campus included the middle school as well as the Juan Cabrillo Elementary School. If the campus burned, it would take all the schools she'd ever attended, not to mention the school where her mother taught. Nina felt helpless when she thought of the theatre burning, the place she loved more than any other. It was her second home.

Furious at her friends, Nina returned to her mother, and her father was there now too. She hugged him, happy to see him alive and uninjured, but John was distraught.

"It's fucked," he said, by way of delivering the news that their home was gone. "The entire hillside was on fire. I had to drive away. There was nothing I could do."

Nina was saddened but glad that the pump had failed. Her father would have stayed otherwise. "The pump breaking saved his life," she told me.

But her father was devastated by the loss of the log cabin home and haunted by the failure of the pump, as though he himself had failed. I could relate. My pump had also failed. If my wife hadn't researched how to hook up to a fire hydrant the night before on YouTube, we would have lost our home as well.

Over the succeeding weeks, while the family stayed at a hotel in Oxnard, Nina found it hard to be around her father, who couldn't get over it. Every conversation seemed to be about "the stupid pump."

Her mother would cry too, but not because she'd lost her home. Jennifer cried when she thought of the animals who lost theirs, as nearly ninety percent of the Santa Monica Mountains was soot and ash. The trails Nina had hiked her whole life were gone.

"We lost a lot," her mother told her. "But we were lucky to have had what we did."

Nina tried to adopt her mother's philosophy as she shopped at thrift stores to find clothes to replace those she'd lost. She no longer cared about getting into the best acting school. She considered taking a gap year, or maybe not acting at all—or ever again.

"Everything seems so fragile," she told me, "and pointless as well."

When Jennifer returned to the classroom six weeks after the fire, five students in her AP English class had lost their homes. Every class had at least two or three kids whose homes were gone.

And it wasn't just the structure that had burned.

In most cases, like her own, everything the kids had ever owned was gone. Every heirloom, every card or letter, every photo album, every stitch of clothing, *everything.*

Teachers adjusted the curriculum to help students cope. One assignment was to write about their home or a special room in it. Some students were willing to go there, many weren't.

"You have to rebuild," Nina told her parents whenever the subject came up. "That has to be my home again."

But it wasn't so simple. Six months after the fire, Jennifer and John were still trying to determine if their home's concrete foundation could be saved. If not, they wouldn't have enough money from insurance.

"It's just stuff," people would say, perhaps to convince themselves. But that didn't ward off the long, difficult, and stressful process of rebuilding. One resident, Randy Nauert, passed away only months after losing his home. Randy, a bass player in one of the very first surf bands, The Challengers, was overwhelmed by the bureaucratic challenges of starting a life over. While his death won't be counted as a casualty of the Woolsey Fire, there is little doubt it is one.

Like Randy, John was really struggling after the fire. When I reached out to him to discuss an interview, he responded with kind notes explaining that he wasn't ready yet. When I checked in a few months later, he no longer responded.

Jennifer said he told her, "I don't know how we are going to get through this."

It was hard for Nina to see her parents under this kind of duress. Her father had built their home with his hands. Now he was throwing them up in defeat.

When I asked Nina if she wished she'd grabbed something from the only bedroom she'd ever known, she said, "I wish I'd taken a picture of my room so I'd remember what was there. Forgetting what once was, that's the saddest part for me."

And then she continued. "I don't think I'll ever be that attached to anything again. I don't think I'll ever have children."

In February, three months after the fire, Malibu High finally presented their annual fall musical, ironically entitled *Spring Awakening*. The show had been scheduled to run for three nights the weekend after the fire. But now the winter's heavy rains and mudslide concerns limited the show to one night. Since my son was in the musical, along with Nina, I knew how many hours he'd spent rehearsing with the cast starting in October. I knew how frustrating it must have been to get only one performance after all that work.

On the opening (and closing) night of *Spring Awakening*, it seemed everyone in Malibu was in attendance. People who didn't even have children in the school, let alone in the production, came out to show their support. The theatre was packed.

I'd like to say that Nina Gonzalez was the best actor on that stage, or that maybe it was my son. But it was the entire cast, a number of whom had lost their homes. Any one of them could've quit and the show would've been cancelled, but they all continued.

At the curtain call, audience members stood cheering and sobbing. I was right there with them. The young people on that stage had produced something as magical as it was ephemeral. And while the production of *Spring Awakening* would be short lived, the community they had created in Malibu would not be.

John Gonzalez in front of the remains of the home he built.
PHOTO DAVE TEEL

The burned down home of the Mehring family.
PHOTO ROBERT KERBECK

6

A TEACHER'S STORY

Patti Mehring has been teaching the kindergarteners of Malibuites for twenty years, including my son, Davis. She and her husband, Wolter, live down the street from us in Malibu Park, a neighborhood of 275 homes. Their thirty-year-old son, Nate, fixed my surfboards.

On the morning of the fire, Patti heard only one bullhorn calling for evacuation. In past fires, sheriffs would drive up and down the street repeatedly ordering residents to leave. What do you pack when you don't have much time? Because it's hard to think straight, *what do you remember to pack?*

When it was time to go, the Mehrings' white terrier mix, Maggie, wouldn't come. An already skittish rescue dog, she was freaked out by the danger she must have sensed and ran away. The family called and searched but they couldn't find her. On the horizon—and aptly named Horizon Drive—the orange glow from the fire grew brighter. Black clouds took over the sky. Patti put out food and water for Maggie hoping she'd come. Nothing. Finally, left with little choice, the family evacuated.

In the Zuma Beach parking lot with thousands of others, Patti and Wolter watched flames from the beach. They heard explosions they assumed were homes going up. Around noon, Wolter snuck in on foot to check on the property. A number of other Malibu Park residents did the same thing, walking in the middle of the street to avoid the flames on both sides of the road. The idea was to get to their places immediately after the initial firestorm had passed through, a strategy the fire department called "fire front following." Then, if their homes were still standing, they could put out spot fires to protect it from stray embers. Unfortunately, the Mehring home was already gone when Wolter made it back. Even in his grief at losing everything he owned, he called and searched for Maggie. He feared she'd hidden under the house and was consumed by the fast-moving flames.

With no home to return to, the family left the city, unaware they wouldn't be allowed to return for over a week. To prevent looting, the LA County Sheriff's Department had set up roadblocks to prevent anyone from getting into Malibu, even residents. For the next days, Patti posted regularly on social media, hoping that someone had seen her dog. She asked locals who'd stayed behind to leave food for her on the property. Many did.

Patti and Wolter tried multiple times to get back into Malibu but the sheriffs turned them away. Nate and his fiancé, Jackie, tried as well but they were also rejected. The only ones allowed past the roadblocks were first responders—and the press.

On Wednesday, nearly a week after the fire, Patti and Wolter hatched a plan to ride into Malibu with a friend, who was an LA County lifeguard. Though the lifeguard would be in his personal vehicle and not an LA County truck, they hoped his identification would be enough to get them through the checkpoints. They wanted to search for Maggie and a safe on their property containing rare coins. Nate and Jackie decided to come along too.

Patti and Jackie rode with their lifeguard friend, while Nate drove his Jeep with his father in the passenger seat. At the checkpoint, manned by three sheriffs, dozens of residents were standing around their cars hoping a friendly sheriff might let them pass. Since no one knew when the authorities were going to allow citizens to "repopulate" (their term for letting people back into Malibu), residents spent hours, sometimes days, waiting for any chance to get home.

The lifeguard pulled up and flashed his identification. "I'm dropping off supplies," he said.

Jackie waited for the lifeguard to tell the sheriff that the Jeep was with them—as they'd planned—but he didn't mention the other vehicle. She figured he knew what he was doing and remained quiet.

"Okay, you can go," said the sheriff.

The lifeguard started through the checkpoint, then seemed to remember Nate and Wolter were behind him. He stopped and yelled out from his window, "Uh, they're with us."

The residents had been watching the interaction and reacted immediately. One lady ran over to the sheriffs, yelling, "My cat's at home. I don't get to see my cat. Why are they getting in?"

"I can't do this," the sheriff said to the lifeguard. "All these people are watching. This is turning into a real peanut gallery."

Nate felt like it was his fault. If he and Jackie had gone in the lifeguard's vehicle, they all would've gotten past the checkpoint. Unlike his parents, who wanted to search for Maggie and then leave, Nate and Jackie were planning to stay overnight at the property. The couple weren't bothered by the lack of electricity or safe drinking water. They had loaded their Jeep with supplies. Because of their extra car, however, the entire group was now in jeopardy of being told to turn around.

Jackie got out and ran to the Jeep, urging Wolter to switch places with her so he could get back home. It was his house, after all. The sheriffs looked extremely unhappy at the switcheroo. Residents went ballistic, shouting at the sheriffs—and the group. Finally, the lifeguard pulled away as Nate and Jackie made a U-turn away from Malibu.

"We blew it," Nate said, frustrated at himself for not thinking to load the supplies from the Jeep into the lifeguard's vehicle. Now he would be unable to help his parents. Heavy rains were in the forecast and the family home was susceptible to flooding. Nate wanted to clear the drains at the property of any debris. He wanted to be sure that whatever valuables not destroyed by the fire weren't then lost in the mud.

His parents spent a few hours at the home, but they couldn't find Maggie or the safe. Nate suspected it was buried somewhere in the remains of the home—unless the safe had been looted, a distinct possibility. On the Nextdoor website, there were dozens of posts about looters sneaking into Malibu via side roads and dirt trails, often on motorcycles.

Nate realized that while the sheriffs were blocking the roads into the city, they weren't watching the ocean. Nate and Jackie had a two-person kayak. They would paddle up the coast. As darkness fell the following day, the couple drove to Sunset and the PCH where the first checkpoint was. They parked the Jeep so that it was out of the view of the sheriffs. They didn't want to be spotted and told to go home—or get arrested.

Wearing wetsuits, they carried the kayak down the wooden staircase to the beach. The moon was out, which made it easier to see. They loaded the kayak with two garbage bags full of food and strapped on four 2½ gallon water containers. Jackie carried a backpack with their phones and a set of clothing for each of them. Jackie got in the front; Nate took the rear.

Their plan was to stop at the La Costa Beach Club in eastern Malibu to bring food to a friend, Tom. He lived in the La Costa neighborhood above the beach and had stayed behind with his wife and father-in-law. Membership was a perk of buying a home in the neighborhood. The beach club consisted of a playground on the sand, a beach volleyball court, a ping-pong table, showers, and a kitchen. There were tables and benches for members to barbeque meals for parties and get-togethers. Even though eastern Malibu hadn't burned, it was under the same evacuation order as the rest of the city. The sheriffs were not only blocking people from entering the city, they were blocking supplies as well.

The five-mile paddle to La Costa was taxing, even for two fit individuals. Whenever Nate and Jackie passed by one of the many canyons in Malibu, the off-shore winds would pick up, threatening to push the kayak out to sea. Lifeguards were often called in for rescues during off-shore conditions since many kayakers ended up in the shipping lanes off the coast. But Nate and Jackie were experienced ocean-goers. Nate was more worried about the winds tipping over the kayak, which was awkwardly weighted under the load of two people, water, and food.

Two exhausting hours later they made it. But the surf had picked up in the meantime, and three- to five-foot waves exploded on the shore sounding like cracks of a whip. Nate feared they would lose their supplies.

Timing the paddle in the dark was tricky. They waited outside the surf zone, trying to read the waves and hoping for a lull. Finally, they went for it and paddled like crazy. When they got close enough to the beach to stand, Jackie jumped into the water with her backpack held high. She grabbed one of the trash bags. Nate hopped out with the other bag in one hand, while holding onto the kayak with the other. But the surf was too strong. The kayak was ripped from his hand and hurtled toward the beach. When they got to it, two of the water containers were gone.

Nate and Jackie hurriedly pulled the kayak onto the sand, in case a sheriff was in the vicinity—or a beach club member mistook them for looters.

Steve Haddix was at the beach club that night, though he wasn't a member. He was a certified firefighter from Oregon and the COO of Atira Systems, which marketed one of Steve's own inventions, a fire-blocking gel called Strong Water. He created the firm to market the gel along with private fire-protection services. He and his "Gel Strike Team," which included four engines and twelve men, had been hired to defend the homes of famous celebrities in Malibu.

Unlike Nate and Jackie who had to sneak in, Steve and his team had "red cards" that allowed them past the roadblocks. Officially known as an Incident Qualification Card, the cards were generated from a training and qualification database run by federal and state agencies that worked in cooperation with the National Wildfire Coordinating Group (NWCG). Red cards are issued only to individuals who'd successfully completed the training, experience, and physical fitness tests required by the agencies that were members of the NWCG. Having a red card meant the individual arriving at a wildfire incident was qualified to do the job—whatever that might be.

Steve had also registered Atira Systems with the Woolsey Fire's Incident Command Center to get permission to be in the area. Because Steve had the blessing of the authorities, roadblocks weren't an issue for them.

Atira Systems had been hired by a La Costa homeowner to defend the man's multimillion-dollar estate. Since the fire hadn't made it to eastern Malibu, however, Steve and three of his men were in wait-and-see mode. Their other engines and firefighters were stationed closer to the action in western Malibu, though none of the homes they were hired to protect saw any flame infringement.

Steve told me that when he and his team met Nate and Jackie at the beach club, they were "amazed they'd paddled as far as they had." Because of the couple's ordeal, the men invited them to dinner. Two of the firefighters, Clarence and Tanner, were from the Warm Springs Reservation in Oregon. They were making a Native American meal of fry bread served with butter and honey and a "side of steak" on the club's barbeque.

The couple wasn't sure if it was the randomness of the encounter that made the meal taste so good but it didn't matter. In the midst of a disaster, they had made new friends. The group spent the night discussing firefighting politics—and celebrities.

In his engine, Steve was carrying a $25,000 bottle of wine for Leonardo DiCaprio. He'd been entrusted with the bottle by a film producer whose home Steve was protecting. The producer wanted to get the wine to Leo for his birthday, which was November 11. Steve could get in and out of the area, something Leo's team wasn't able to do. But when Steve went to make the drop, Leo's team was a no-show. Steve had been carrying the birthday present for days since. Once, he opened the door to his truck and the bottle rolled out onto the ground. His heart sank, but somehow the bottle didn't break. He wanted to be rid of it and briefly considered sharing it with the group.

Steve found a drink was usually necessary whenever he discussed firefighting politics. He felt union cronyism was blocking new technologies like his from being accepted by the firefighting community, especially in California. His

Strong Water gel eliminated the issue of rekindle. The product also reduced the issues of structural collapse and the risk of steam burn by limiting the amount of water needed and reducing the weight load. The gel was more environmentally friendly than the Class A foams typically used by fire departments in California. He felt the use of his product could have saved many homes. The leader in the production of retardants and gels was Perimeter Solutions, known for the manufacture of Phos-Chek, the chemical I sprayed on my home. Steve wondered if the fact that Perimeter Solutions was based in California had anything to do with their domination of the local market.

Nate and Jackie told stories too, of there being no firefighters in Malibu Park. Nate wouldn't have left if he'd known no one would protect his home. He'd already decided he was staying for the next fire.

Early the following morning, it was back to the ocean. Nate and Jackie borrowed a rescue board from the beach club to reduce the weight on the kayak. The ten-foot board was basically an extra-long surfboard. With Nate in the kayak and Jackie paddling the rescue board, they were able to move more quickly. An hour later, they arrived at the Malibu Pier and First Point, one of the most famous waves in the world. Nate took the kayak into the beach. He hoped to find someone willing to drive them fifteen minutes up the highway to his parents' home. Jackie spotted two surfers in the lineup, when there would normally be fifty and couldn't resist surfing a few waves.

On the beach, Nate chatted with a lifeguard, who didn't seem particularly concerned that the couple had snuck into Malibu.

"Those guys out there surfing," the lifeguard said, "have a killer boat. Maybe you can catch a ride with them." He explained that the men were off-duty lifeguards from the South Bay area who'd boated up to help.

One of the guys surfing with Jackie caught a wave in.

"I'm with that girl out there," Nate told him. "Any chance you guys can give us a ride to Zuma?"

"Hell yeah. No problem. We're waiting for another boat to bring us supplies, then we'll go."

Nate figured he might as well catch a few waves while waiting and took the rescue board when Jackie brought it in. But it wasn't enjoyable. He couldn't stop thinking about the burned homes, many of which were visible in the hills. Huge swaths of the Santa Monica Mountains were charred black.

When the boat was ready to go, they loaded the kayak and rescue board. The boat dropped them at Zuma Beach since that was the closest place for them to walk home, but Jackie said the surf was "freakier in the day than the beach club had been at night." Zuma was known for having a pounding shore break and for punishing surfers, even advanced ones. It was not known for cumbersome watercraft like two-person kayaks.

They started toward shore, aware that they were risking arrest. While the lifeguard at First Point didn't seem to care, the lifeguards at Zuma Beach might feel differently. Not only was Zuma Beach the headquarters for the entire area, it had also served as the main evacuation point during the fire.

But Nate felt the sheriff's department had given them no other choice. Some residents had created fake press passes to get in. If it was safe for hundreds of reporters and news vans to enter Malibu and traipse over the remains of people's homes, why couldn't residents return? Especially ones trying to find their dog.

Because Nate was by himself in the kayak, he was able to maneuver faster and make it in without being wiped out. Jackie got in safely on the rescue board too.

When they made it to the sand, three lifeguards were waiting. They didn't seem pleased to see them—or their kayak. "You're not allowed to be here," one of them said. "But we're not going to tell you to go."

This was good news since Nate didn't think he could get the kayak back out through the surf, which was pumping. They dragged their stuff up the beach to the parking lot.

Now what? He wondered. *Do we leave the kayak? Our food?*

No way could they carry it up the steep hills of Malibu Park to get to their home. Just then, an old guy with shock white hair and wearing farmer overalls pulled up in an old F350 truck.

"I watched you come in," he said. "You're going to get arrested by the sheriffs if they see you with that kayak." The sheriffs, nearly all of whom were from outside of Malibu, didn't like their rules to be circumvented. "Throw it in the truck bed," the old guy said.

Nate and Jackie hustled to hide the evidence of their crime as quickly as possible.

"We're going to make a stop first." The old guy drove them to the other end of the parking lot where a pop-up T-Mobile store had been created, complete with a hot pink banner. The company had set up a mobile cell tower to ensure service for its customers since most towers were melted in the fire. Jackie and Nate were handed free phones that came fully charged, along with power banks for when the phones ran low. Smoke was still visible in the hills.

"It was like a ghost town with swag," said Jackie.

The old guy tried to drive them home, but the sheriff on Busch Drive wouldn't let them pass, not even when Nate showed his valid driver's license with his home address on it.

"No," said the sheriff, refusing to discuss the matter. The roadblocks weren't just on the outskirts of the city—they were on every street. The group drove to other access points into the neighborhood. They were turned away time and again. Finally, they tried the only other way in. The sheriff on Guernsey Avenue took pity on them and let them through.

Much of Malibu Park was still smoldering from railroad ties which continued to burn a week after the fire. Nate and Jackie had been texted photos of the burned-down family home so they knew what to expect. Still, it was difficult to block their emotions when they first saw the rubble. It was one thing to be told the home was gone, but it was something else to see it in person. The chimney was the only thing standing.

Mourning had to wait, though, and so they went right into action mode. Nate found the safe buried amongst the debris and dragged it to a neighbor's house two doors down. Most of the rare coins inside—which included silver dollars, gold coins, a bar of silver—were burned. The plastic holders surrounding them had been melted. The coins would never again be considered mint. Some had been fused together by the heat. The couple searched the property for anything else that might have made it but found very little. Twice, sheriffs' cars stopped at the house to verify that Nate and Jackie weren't looters.

And then a third sheriff pulled up.

"What's going on here?" he shouted as he got out of his cruiser.

In the distance, Jackie heard a faint sound, but she was focused on the approaching sheriff. The sound came closer and closer until she realized it was the barking of a dog.

"Maggie," she screamed and ran away without answering the sheriff's question.

From beneath their next door neighbor's house, one of the few in the neighborhood still standing, Maggie trotted out. She seemed unharmed, though she was no longer white due to the black ash and soot from the fire. She was also no longer quite so skittish. Apparently, she'd had enough of living by herself in the wasteland of Malibu Park and came directly to them. Nate and Jackie were so happy to have a happy moment in the midst of so much devastation.

Even the sheriff seemed pleased. "Wait, you just found your dog after a week?"

The family renamed her "Miracle Maggie."

One month later, the schools in Malibu were finally opening again and Patti prepared to return to teaching her kindergartners. She was desperate to take a break from the misery of her loss. She didn't want to talk about it when people asked her whether she would rebuild since she, like so many others, wasn't sure she had enough insurance. She was hurt there'd been no firefighters in Malibu Park on the morning of the fire, but more than that, she believed they didn't care about the community. In the past, she said firefighters drove around to make sure each home had the required brush clearance, the monitoring of which was the responsibility of the LA County Fire Department. But she hadn't seen them do that for over a decade.

The overgrown brush, as well as the lack of firefighters, had led to the staggering number of homes lost in the neighborhood. Already, she was forgetting what the homes she'd driven by countless times looked like.

The day before school started again, the teachers went through trauma training. They were instructed to focus on the social and emotional aspects of recovery, putting education in the background. Patti's entire class of fourteen had been evacuated. Two children had lost their homes and one didn't come back because the parents were concerned about the air quality in the area, even though their home had survived.

While the elementary school didn't burn, the fire had come right to the edge of the campus, which also included the only middle and high school in Malibu. Though none of the schools were damaged, they stood directly below the three streets that had lost the most homes. Each morning it seemed the smell of smoke was stronger, rather than weaker. Whenever the Santa Ana winds blew again, which they did often, they drove toxic ash and soot to the schools. Teachers, staff, and students were breathing the remains of refrigerators, washers, dryers, stereo systems, insulation materials, chemicals, tools, and anything else that couldn't withstand 2,000-degree heat.

Of the twenty teachers and staff members at Juan Cabrillo Elementary, eight had lost their homes. Returning to work was a way for the adults to put the tragedy in the back of their minds, at least for a few hours. On the first day, the children were given a chance to talk about their experiences in what the teachers called "sharing time."

But the children didn't want to talk. They wanted to play with their friends, many of whom they'd known all their short lives. Patti could tell the children were changed by the fire, but she was experienced enough to follow their lead and let them share in their own time and way.

Still, she heard things those first days that shook her.

"I used to have a Christmas tree, but it burned," one child said.

"My scissors got melted," said another.

On the third day back, while the children were playing in the pretend kitchen, she heard a child say, "Fire, there's a fire."

"We need to evacuate," said another child.

Working together, the children took every item from the pretend kitchen and moved it across the room. Instead of being scary, it seemed therapeutic, as if the children were using their play to work out something very real. And they were doing it with their best friends. They repeated the game over and over.

Later that day, their stories poured out of them. The teachers sat and listened as each child told their experience of the fire, often with rich, visual details, as if the fire had turned five-year-olds into thirty-year-olds. Patti felt honored to hear their stories. She realized the ones having the hardest time weren't the kids. Patti told me she flinched whenever she heard a siren. She found herself checking her phone constantly for emergency alerts. In her mind, she ran the school's evacuation procedures over and over again. After all, it was her job to make sure her kids were okay.

But who would watch over the teachers?

HazMat crews removing toxic substances from burned homes.

PHOTO NANCY SAVER

Katie Cook searching for Clover the Tortoise.

PHOTO CHRISTIE TRACY

7

ANIMAL RESCUE

Katie Cook lives in Ojai, California and runs The Little Farm, an animal sanctuary for neglected and discarded farm animals.

Less than a year before the Woolsey Fire, in December 2017, she and her family had fled the Thomas Fire that decimated Santa Barbara and Ventura Counties. The morning of that fire, Katie and her husband, Les, woke up smelling smoke. But there were no alarms or sheriffs shouting for them to evacuate.

Les loaded their two young kids, along with their five dogs, cat, and bunny. He evacuated the kids and the household pets to safety while Katie stayed behind. She was in charge of the other animals they cared for, which included a piglet named Ruby, a mini-horse named Gus, three baby rams, chickens, and ducks. She packed everyone she could into her old Land Cruiser, but Gus wouldn't fit. Desperate, she called Ventura County Animal Services to get a trailer for him since she had loaned hers to a friend, never expecting a fire.

Animal Services was inundated with rescue calls. "We'll come later when we have a trailer available. You should evacuate now though," they told her.

"I'm not leaving without my animal," she said, not willing to leave his fate in the hands of someone else. She waited for Animal Services as the fire crept closer and closer. She wasn't sure who was more afraid—her or the animals—as the sky changed from blue to black. At least, she hadn't relieved herself inside the Land Cruiser as most of the animals had due to the stress. Their instincts were to flee from danger and here she was sitting with them, stuck in her truck.

When Animal Services finally showed up and loaded Gus seven hours later, their convoy needed a police escort to make it out safely. On Highway 33, flames covered both sides of the road. While it was the most frightening moment of her life, she also found the colors from the fire "beautiful in some way." I remember my own awe at the speed at which the fire moved, how hard it was to stop marveling at something that could kill me.

Once they made it past the flames, Katie headed north with Gus and all her animals toward the Danish-influenced town of Solvang to meet up with Les and her kids. When she arrived, the Alisal Ranch had set up barn space for animals at no cost for her and other evacuees. The resort marketed itself as a "dude ranch" with over 10,000 acres and fifty miles of riding trails. It was the perfect refuge for her family.

Until the fire came there too.

She packed up her family and menagerie to head further north. Unfortunately, everyone else was doing the same thing. Hotels were booked for miles and the ones that weren't didn't want five dogs, chickens, and hooved animals.

"I promise to keep the pig in the bath," she told one desk clerk. "I'll pay any cleanup fee you want."

No one would take them.

Finally, she spotted the Arroyo Grande Veterinary Clinic, which opened its doors—and an entire wing—to her animals. The clinic didn't even charge her. The next morning, Katie began temporarily distributing her animals to various friends. Fifteen days after the fire, they were allowed to return home to Ojai. Their house was untouched by flames but had suffered significant damage from ash and smoke. The cleanup took weeks.

Katie called 2018 her "regroup" year. By the fall, things were looking up. Intakes to her sanctuary had quadrupled. So when Katie heard about the Woolsey Fire, she thought, *oh no, here we go again.*

As the news got worse that Friday morning, Katie wanted to be of service. She'd experienced the generosity of others in her time of need and wanted to repay those favors. She went to the Humane Society of Ventura County office in Ojai with her truck and a trailer. "Let me help," she said. "I went through the Thomas Fire. I know what people need. I know what animals need even better."

Normally, the Humane Society handles only dogs, cats, and horses but during an emergency they open their doors to all animals. Katie knew that partnering with the Humane Society would enable her to access the fire areas since humane officers are considered first responders and are allowed past roadblocks. The director of the society, Jolene Hoffman, welcomed Katie's help, though she did give pause when she noticed Katie was wearing a walking boot on her left foot from a recent surgery.

A few hours later, a caravan of Humane Society vehicles headed toward Agoura Hills to rescue horses at a ranch where there weren't enough trailers. In the lead was a white van with two Humane Society officers, Kendra Winwood and Tracy Vail, followed by three trucks each with an attached trailer. Two of the trucks had sheriffs' decals to allow them past the roadblocks. Katie was in the rear with her Land Cruiser, hoping the sheriffs wouldn't object to her tagging along.

She made it through without being stopped.

When the group arrived at the horse property, the flames that were closing in gave her Thomas Fire flashbacks. As Katie and the others piled out of their vehicles, embers and flying debris whipped past them driven by the demonic winds. The team steered frightened horses to the trailers, managing to keep them calm enough to get them inside. Coughing and squinting, they raced to their vehicles and quickly drove off. If they'd gotten there any later, the horses would have burned to death. Katie and the team took the rescued horses back to Ojai that night to stay at the Humane Society for as long as they needed.

In the morning, the team headed to Malibu and Zuma Beach. On the drive down the PCH, the sign welcoming visitors to Malibu was broken and dangling in the wind. Telephone poles were hanging over the cliffs. There were multiple fires and the air was thick with black acrid smoke. Katie saw the same horses, donkeys, and llamas that I did tied to lifeguard towers. They'd been evacuated by their owners, who had spent the night in their nearby cars.

To maximize the number of rescues, the Humane Society split into teams. Equine specialist Christie Tracy led one team with two volunteers: Steve Bower and her boyfriend, Bennie Scorsur. They were standing in the parking lot when an LA County firefighter pulled up in a red Ford F250.

"I've got two burned horses up on Horizon Drive," the firefighter shouted.

While Christie was in charge of the horses, Steve was in charge of the driving. In his mid-fifties and a semitruck driver by trade, he'd driven for the Humane Society during the Thomas Fire to rescue countless large animals.

"I'll go with the firefighter," Steve told Christie, "to see if it's possible to get a trailer up there."

Half an hour later, he returned. "It's gonna be tight, but I think I can make it."

Steve hopped into his Dodge Ram truck, which was pulling a trailer that could hold four horses. Christie and Bennie got in too. Just then a news crew from ABC7 showed up.

"Hey," Steve yelled. "We're going to rescue two burned horses. Might make a pretty good story." He revved the engine and took off.

The news van followed on their tail.

Driving into the Malibu Park neighborhood was "eerie." Downed power lines zigzagged the roads. Abandoned cars sat in the middle of the street. Fires still burned on the hillsides. If anyone could avoid the debris and get them in and out safely, though, it was Steve.

When they reached the property, which bordered National Parks land at the top of the neighborhood, the view of the ocean was almost as staggering as the destruction they found. The cars on the property had melted. One was a pickup truck. No structures remained standing anywhere within view. The ground was still hot from the flames. In the distance, Christie saw a pasture with a burned white vinyl fence. Inside what remained of the corral were the two horses.

Even from a hundred yards away, she could tell they needed serious medical attention.

"They look like they're in respiratory distress," she told the reporter with the news crew.

The pathway to the corral was blocked by a web of tangled power lines. Bennie used sticks to move them out of the way, trying not to get electrocuted.

When Christie reached the horses, whose names she would later learn were Pepe and Flash, it was clear Pepe was in much worse shape. His face looked to be three times its normal size. His body had char marks. The hairs on his tail and mane were curled up from having been burned. Pepe's air passages were constricted and closing fast.

Someone had tried to get a halter on the animal but put it on backwards. The halter was now burned into the horse's skin. Christie grew up on a 6,500-acre ranch in Ventura County and had never seen anything like it, not even in the Thomas Fire. She had no idea how to interact with an animal so badly injured. Christie and Bennie grabbed lead ropes from the horse trailer and approached the animals. The horses were apprehensive but seemed ready to go. They'd been without food or water for over twenty-four hours.

Bennie put a lead rope on Flash and led him around the dangling power lines toward the trailer.

Christie put a rope on Pepe. "Come on, bud," she said. "Let's get you out of here."

Pepe followed Flash and the two made it to the trailer. But Flash got spooked and wouldn't go inside. Christie was afraid the horse was going to bolt and that Pepe might run too. If Pepe didn't receive immediate attention, he was going to die.

"Let's try Pepe first," she told Bennie. She walked into the trailer and held up some hay. Though Pepe's lips were burned, he was too hungry not to eat. He went inside and Flash followed.

When they returned to Zuma Beach, Christie was desperate to get Pepe to a veterinarian right away, but officials with the Humane Society wanted to unload Pepe and Flash from the four-horse trailer and put them in a two-horse trailer.

"We need to use our space better," said the head of the Humane Society, Jolene Hoffman.

"No, we gotta go now," said Christie. "This horse isn't going to make it."

She was sure each moment that delayed treatment made it more likely Pepe would die.

By a stroke of luck, a veterinarian, Allie Tashnek, was in the parking lot. She and her boyfriend, Chris Weber, had come to help.

"I need you to look at this horse," Christie said.

As Allie examined Pepe, Weber noticed the backwards halter.

"Hey," he said, "you put this on backwards."

"Are you kidding me?" Christie snapped, her anguish about Pepe's injuries spilling out at Weber. "We *found* him that way. We gotta get him to Somis."

Somis is a tiny town half an hour away. The "downtown" is one street. But it had the only equine hospital in the area.

"My trailer is empty," Allie said. "I can take both horses right now."

Spacing issues solved, Jolene Hoffman agreed.

The news footage of the burned horses went viral. The niece of the elderly owner of the animals reached out to the Humane Society and was put into contact with Christie.

"Is there still a house?" the niece asked.

"Not to my knowledge," said Christie.

"Did you happen to see two chocolate Labs?"

"No, there were no dogs on the property. The firefighter would've said something if he saw them."

"They were tethered in the back of the pickup truck."

Christie recalled the melted pickup she'd seen on the property. Could the dogs have been inside? Sick to her stomach, she checked a photo Bennie had taken. In the background, she could see the truck but not inside the vehicle. She was going to have to go back there.

Around the same time Christie was rescuing Pepe and Flash, Katie Cook got a call from Jillian Dempsey, a Malibu Park resident who was overseas when the fire broke out. Jillian was jumping on a return flight but needed someone to rescue her animals, which included donkeys, goats, chickens, bunnies, a large pot-bellied pig, and a one-hundred pound tortoise.

Katie tried to get her Land Cruiser up into the neighborhood but, in the dark, it was impossible to find her way through the destruction covering the streets. Even if she somehow made it to the home, pulling out frightened large animals at night was a very bad idea.

"I promise first light I'll get your animals," Katie told Jillian.

At home in Ojai that night, Katie printed out the maps Jillian had drawn of her property, which included the locations of the animals. But when the Humane Society caravan arrived in the morning, the home had burned in the fire and the maps were useless. The street looked like a war zone. It seemed every house was destroyed. Some of the animals had escaped through holes the fire had burned in their fences. One chicken coop was gone entirely. The team loaded the remaining chickens and rabbits first. It was near impossible to catch some of the terrified animals. One rabbit screamed when Katie caught it.

The group then focused on the donkeys and goats. Katie wasn't wearing a mask since she "didn't want the animals to be scared of her on top of already being scared." To the animals, she was a stranger trying to capture them. They needed to see her face and be able to hear her voice as she tried to corral them. The animals had been traumatized by what they'd lived through. The last thing she wanted was to add to that trauma.

Still, the animals had to be moved to safety. The air quality was far from safe; it was potentially deadly. Homes had melted to the ground, along with everything inside them—electronics, refrigerators, cars, toxic paint, and building materials. After a few hours, Katie could feel the toll the air was taking on her lungs. The animals had been breathing those toxins for days. So when one goat made a run for an opening in the fence, Katie went Superwoman to catch it, leaping through the air to grab onto its hock. Another Humane Society employee had the same idea. He leapt too, landing directly on top of Katie—and her recently operated-on foot.

The rabbit wasn't the only one who screamed that day.

After she shook off the pain and the donkeys and goats were loaded, it was time to rescue Hank the pig. To move the 400-pound pig she had to convince the animal it would be fun to take a walk. Hands on his butt, she nudged him to safety.

Clover, the tortoise, was last. Katie had promised she wouldn't leave one animal behind, but finding the tortoise was quite the challenge. The owner had warned Katie that Clover liked to dig and might have gone underground. Katie was shocked by the size of the hole she discovered. It looked like a construction crew had excavated for a small pool. At first, she wasn't sure the animal was even in the hole. The only way to know was to climb down, bad foot and all.

The team lowered her head first. The hole was littered with the bodies of sparrows and mice killed in the fire. Once Katie got to the bottom, she could see a tunnel. Clover had dug a massive hole and a tunnel system as well. Putting her head inside the opening, she came face-to-face with Clover, alive and well in his burrow.

I know what to do, the animal seemed to say. *I'm okay. Go save the others.*

She could tell Clover was dug in. Extracting the tortoise could potentially collapse the tunnel. Katie had food and water brought down, then took all the other animals to safety.

On Monday, Christie returned to the Horizon Drive property, this time with Humane Society Officer Kendra Winwood. In the bed of the pickup, the women found only bones. They couldn't even tell what the breed was.

"I'd never broken down before," said Winwood, "until I saw that."

Because the dogs had been tied up, they were unable to escape. Christie had worked with animals her entire life, and in all her experiences in both the Thomas and Woolsey Fires, she had never seen a situation where an animal was set free and didn't survive. If you had to leave and couldn't take your animals, you let them go.

During the succeeding days, the Humane Society was involved in a series of difficult calls with the owner and other family members.

"Did you know what you were doing when you locked those animals in?" Christie asked.

"I thought they would be safe," the owner said, a common refrain (and mistake) of those who left animals behind.

When I asked why the owner hadn't taken the dogs with her when she evacuated, Winwood said, "There wasn't time" and "All of a sudden the fire was there." She urges animal owners to have go bags ready with at least five days of food and water in an airtight container, along with any medicines. A carrier with blankets and towels (and a familiar toy) is also critical since pets can behave strangely during a disaster. She stressed the importance of having an evacuation plan and knowing where you can take your animals since many hotels and evacuation centers might not take pets.

Complicating the interaction with the owner was a GoFundMe page set up by a friend of the family to raise money for veterinary costs and hospital bills, except the family already knew the Humane Society was covering all of those costs. The page raised thousands of dollars, which left "a bad taste" for Christie. An update on the site said anything over the costs would be donated to the Humane Society. Since there weren't any costs, that money should have been donated. To date, the Humane Society hasn't received a penny.

While the owner had done nothing illegal, the Humane Society was concerned about returning the horses. Pepe and Flash needed constant care. The owner had a life to rebuild since she'd lost everything. At first, the owner was taken aback by the suggestion of giving up her horses. She broke down in tears during one conference call. But eventually she accepted that the horses would be better off in a new home. Pepe and Flash were adopted by a rescue facility and are living out their days in luxury on twenty-five acres. Rescue workers like Christie Tracy and Officer Winwood didn't consider their job done until evacuated animals were returned to a home that was safe.

Katie Cook wasn't done after the fires either. For her, it wasn't enough that she had rescued hundreds of animals. She wanted to be sure they returned to full health. For months afterwards, she went to the Humane Society twice a day to feed the animals she'd saved. The heavy rains that followed the Woolsey Fire caused mudslides, complicating her efforts to return the animals. The mudslides that followed the Thomas Fire had killed over twenty people and Katie wasn't losing any of her animals.

Finally, three months after the fire, she took them back to Malibu. The chickens immediately went to work inspecting their new and improved coops while looking for bugs and taking dirt baths. All of the animals looked relieved to be in an open and sunny space.

Clover climbed out of his hole to welcome them home.

Pepe and Flash

PHOTO CHRISTIE TRACY

Tanesha Lockhart inside her car recording her "goodbye" video.
PHOTO TANESHA LOCKHART

8

THE LA MODEL

On the Friday of the Woolsey Fire, Bruce Bates was up at 4:30 a.m. doing his yoga stretching routine and preparing for the start of his 6:00 a.m. shift. A deputy probation officer (DPO) with the Los Angeles County Probation Department, Bruce is also a licensed marriage and family therapist with a master's in clinical psychology. The skill set was critical since he worked with juvenile felons, mainly sixteen- and seventeen-year-old boys. Many had been arrested multiple times, often on gun charges. Most were gang members.

Instead of locking kids up and throwing away the key, Los Angeles County had moved toward a philosophy of "compassion and education" when authorities realized they couldn't arrest their way out of the problem. Past offenses like truancy or tagging, which might have landed a young man in a juvenile facility, were no longer prosecuted. As a result, the number of kids in the probation system had dropped over the last few years from approximately 4,000 to 400. Those remaining, however, were often the most challenging, having committed the most serious offenses.

As part of this new way of treating youth, dubbed the "LA Model," detention facilities were changing too. One old prison camp high in the hills of

Malibu's Decker Canyon, Camp Kilpatrick, had been remodeled at a cost of $53 million. The facility was even renamed Campus Kilpatrick, as if it were a small college, rather than a jail for violent young men. Each twenty-four-bed unit was called a cottage instead of a cell block. Campus Kilpatrick had a pool, a gym, basketball courts, and a library. The dorms looked like ski lodges. A culinary school and wood shop rounded out the amenities.

Because Bruce lived in nearby Malibu Park, he had an easy (and stunning) commute to work each morning, driving up steep canyon roads to the campus. Like many families that purchased in the early days of the Malibu real estate industry, the property had been cheap. His parents, Frank and Bonnie, got the home in 1971 for $68,000. Frank was a minister then. Bonnie was a teacher and later became a secretary at Pepperdine University. Western Malibu had been considered the "boonies" then—and still is to a degree, as few want to live so far away from Los Angeles. Because of the smart purchase his parents made—and because the probation department didn't pay much—Bruce had built a guest house on the property and lived there with his wife, Carla, his daughter, Jade, and his son, Declan. His mother still lived in the main house.

When he heard the fire had jumped the 101 Freeway, Bruce's first thought was of the boys at Campus Kilpatrick. "I gotta get the kids out," he told Carla. Because he'd grown up in Malibu and experienced fires before, he figured he'd be driving one of the department's vans to evacuate the youth. "There's no staff up there."

DPOs worked fifty-six hour shifts and normally slept at Campus Kilpatrick but, due to a bed bug infestation in the staff quarters, the DPOs on duty had spent the night at a recently closed detention facility, Camp Gonzales, which was over twenty-five minutes away. The forty-eight youth at Campus Kilpatrick were being supervised only by the night staff. But, unlike the DPOs who had advanced degrees as well as significant training, the night staff were often young and still in college. They had little knowledge of what to do in the case of a major wildfire. Bruce left his family with instructions to evacuate to his sister's place in Oxnard and drove toward the fire.

When he reached Campus Kilpatrick at 5:45 a.m., he went straight to the Administrative Building's control center. On the way up the mountain, he didn't see any flames but the smoke was thick. "Are the kids up yet?" he asked Tanesha Lockhart, the DPO supervisor in charge that morning. She was the only deputized staff who'd remained behind at the facility, sleeping in a chair in the conference room, though she wasn't even supposed to be there. She'd been scheduled to leave early the night before to use Friday to complete errands for her wedding in just over a week.

But the fire had changed everything.

"No, I was waiting for headquarters to tell us whether to evacuate."

"I think we should get everyone up and ready."

"What about breakfast?"

Bruce didn't think there was time but they were dealing with growing boys. Without food, they might be difficult to handle. Already they would be off their meds, as the facility's nurse wasn't going to make it in.

"I'll put the food on trays and bring it to their cottages," he said, worried the normal meal service in the dining hall would take too much time. "They'll eat while they get ready. We gotta get out of here fast."

The hills were beginning to glow. The smoke was making it difficult to breathe too. And just after 7:00 a.m., when the boys were done eating, the power went out and the phone lines went dead.

Moments later, a sheriff pulled up. "The fire's gonna be here in ten minutes. Get out!" He drove off before Bruce could ask for help.

The facility had a number of vans which could hold up to nine youth plus the driver and one staff member. They also had a bus but no one could find the keys.

Because of his knowledge of the local roads, Bruce felt sure he could get a van out. The staff put plastic handcuffs, known as flex cuffs, on nine kids and hustled them into one of the vans, but because they were rushing, many of the cuffs were put on incorrectly. An arriving DPO, Celena Durazo-Kent, joined Bruce's vehicle. He drove off as another van was being filled, aiming for Kanan

Dume Road—his normal route home—but a wall of fire the size of a billboard blocked his path.

"How do we get out?" Celena asked.

"Not that way, for sure," Bruce quipped. He turned around and headed for Encinal Canyon Road. Some of the kids grew agitated. A few had ripped their cuffs off. One new kid was freaking out about the fire and kicking the window, trying to break it. He was six feet tall and weighed 200 well-muscled pounds. Tattoos covered his body, including his neck and hands. He'd only been at Kilpatrick for two weeks. Bruce didn't know what the young man was capable of and drove as quickly as he dared.

Encinal Canyon was safe to drive down though the smoke masked most of his visibility. When Bruce made it to the PCH, he saw flames coming over the ridge in Malibu Park, only a few minutes away.

If I could run up there, I could save my home.

He could also save his family's stuff, which included his grandfather's World War II uniform, photographs of San Francisco and Yosemite from the 1920s, and an old-fashioned piggy bank shaped like a St. Bernard rescue dog. The bank had survived the 1906 San Francisco Fire because it was made of cast iron. He would grab his wife's paintings. He would get the skateboard his son had made for him. On the underside of it, his son had written a note about what a great father Bruce was.

But he was duty bound to stay with the youth first and look after his own family second. Bruce bypassed his home and headed toward Point Dume. When they got there, however, the traffic was jammed. He tried to sneak around the gridlock but every alternate route was congested as well.

He pulled over in the Point Dume neighborhood, home to celebrities and billionaires. He played music to keep the kids calm, which worked with most of them, but the new kid wouldn't stop kicking at the window. He was in a near manic state. Celena used her cell phone to call for an armed unit.

"I want to pee," another boy shouted. "Let me out!"

Bruce empathized. Since he's in his mid-fifties, he found himself needing to pee all the time but feared one (or more) of the youth would make a run for it if he opened the doors. Recapturing them in the chaos of the fire would be impossible. They might head into the hills thinking they wouldn't be spotted and then find themselves in danger either from the fire or the lack of water. He was responsible for keeping them—and his community—safe.

He had to wait for the armed unit.

Up at Campus Kilpatrick, they'd finally found the keys to the bus. Tanesha went to the Aspen cottage to evacuate the twenty-two remaining youth. "You need to move quickly," she said. Ashes swirled into the facility any time someone opened one of the doors. The smell of smoke permeated everything as she loaded the kids into the bus.

Around 8:00 a.m., as the hillside exploded into flames, Fire Engine 72 pulled into the parking lot with Captain Rick Mullen and two firefighters. Mullen's territory stretched from Castro Peak to Leo Carrillo and contained some of the thickest brush in the Santa Monica Mountains. He was also one of Malibu's five city council members.

Earlier he'd received a call that two hikers were trapped at the top along with their dog and took his engine up to Castro Peak. But the conditions on the road were too dangerous. Fire blazing above and below them forced them to turn back. A helicopter was sent to rescue the hikers and Mullen headed to nearby Campus Kilpatrick.

When he arrived, the bus was ready to leave and pointed in the direction where the flames were the worst. A 400-foot cloud of smoke covered the hillside.

"It's too late to evacuate," he told Tanesha. "If you do, I can't guarantee your safety. The best thing now is to shelter in place." Mullen knew from experience that most people didn't evacuate early enough and when they found themselves in trouble, they panicked. That was often how people died, leaving too late and then burning to death in their cars.

Mullen made the decision to shelter in place in part because the campus had something that offered protection against the fire—good brush clearance. The facility sat in a low spot in the hills, giving it good topography as well. Mullen believed the flames would go around or over the facility.

But Tanesha had to make the decision. Whatever happened, it would be her responsibility. "We're going back inside," she said.

One of the bigger kids jumped up from his seat, screaming, "Let's get the fuck out of here. We're gonna die if we don't leave."

She told the boy to sit down. The new probation model depended on building rapport with the youth so she sat beside him. "I'm getting married next week. Trust me, we are getting out of here. We just have to wait until it's safe."

Mullen ordered the bus onto the basketball court in the center of the campus. He had the employees move their personal vehicles from the employee lot to the basketball court as well. Masks were handed out but there weren't enough. Despite her asthma, Tanesha went without one. She was focused on the youth and her staff, not herself. Eyes burning, she ran back and forth between the bus and the control center. Employees not on the bus sat in their cars, engines and air conditioning running. The facility's fire alarm blared incessantly—as if anyone didn't know there was a fire.

At one point, one of the staff members noticed the hood of his vehicle was too hot to touch so all the vehicles were moved to the other end of the court, which was furthest from the approaching flames.

Mullen and his firefighters patrolled the perimeter of the facility. They'd hooked up to a hydrant and were hosing down brush which had caught fire behind one of the buildings. The hillside looked like a volcano full of lava ready to roll downhill and destroy the campus.

Fires started breaking out in the middle of the campus too. Shrubs and landscaping planted as part of the remodel went ablaze, jeopardizing structures. Tanesha ran inside the administration building to grab a fire extinguisher. She passed it to someone outside and ran in to get another, then another. The staff created a "bucket brigade," using the extinguishers to put out spot fires. The smoke was so thick it was hard to breathe. Most of the staff had wetted their shirts and pulled them over their faces to use as makeshift bandanas.

Back on Point Dume, the armed unit made it to Bruce and his van in record time. Because the unit was coming up from Santa Monica, not a single car was on that side of the road. Everyone was trying to get *out* of Malibu, not *in*.

The flashing lights of the vehicle, however, along with its three armed guards, seemed to reinvigorate the kid in the van. He started kicking at the window again.

"Hey, we're not your regular probation officers," one of the guards said as he approached the boy. "We don't play around."

"Where I come from," the kid said, "we don't play around either."

The guard had a gun as well as pepper spray and appeared ready to use at least one on the boy.

"I'll deal with the kid," Bruce said, stepping in between them. "You figure out how to get us the hell out of here."

When the guard walked away, Bruce turned calmly to the boy. "I'm losing all my shit today. My house is burning down. If you could give me a break, I'd appreciate it."

The kid kicked at the window one more time, then stopped.

When Tanesha couldn't take the smoke anymore, she climbed inside her vehicle and quickly shut the door. Outside it looked like night, except for the flames that appeared to be a hundred feet tall. Even with the doors and windows closed, she could hear trees snapping and the brush crackling as the fire consumed everything in its path.

She realized she might not make it out alive. So she grabbed her phone and began to record a video.

"Okay, everybody, I want to let you guys know I love you. I know you aren't able to communicate with me, but I believe in God and I'm comfortable right now."

She flipped the camera around to show her family what was happening outside her car window. It looked like the tornado scene in the black and white opening *of The Wizard of Oz.* Other than the flames, no color existed anywhere. Everything was gray—or black.

"The fire department says we're in the safest place. The wind is blowing heavily. I can't breathe outside."

She addressed her fiancé, "Billy, I love you." And then she turned off her phone.

She went back to the bus to check on the youth. They were quiet. Even the class clowns were speechless. When she tried to make a joke, one of them just shook his head. Nothing was funny about this fire. It seemed to her the boys had accepted that they were going to die. For a split second, the sun broke through.

Thank you, God, she thought.

But it disappeared again, and the skies grew darker.

Okay, now wait a minute.

Moments later, the sun came out again. This time, it stayed. After three hours of sheltering in place, which "felt like an eternity," the storm had passed.

A big cheer came from the bus. The kids and staff—and the $53 million facility—were safe.

"The fire has passed through," Mullen told Tanesha. "Someone is coming to escort you out." He explained his engine was now needed elsewhere.

Ten minutes after Mullen and his men left, a sheriff arrived to escort the bus to a probation facility in Ventura County. Bruce Bates had made it there too, following the armed unit, lights flashing the entire way. The other van made it too. Sadly, Bruce's home was lost in the fire. So was his mother's.

"We could've saved the house," Declan told his father when they returned to the property two days later. Concrete pilings had been ripped from the ground. It looked like a bomb went off. The firenado that came through Malibu Park had hit their home head on. Most of the remains were smoldering and still hot from the flames. The St. Bernard bank was the only thing that survived.

Declan didn't say anything else. He was shut down for weeks afterwards. For him, staying behind was a manhood thing. Bruce's one regret was that he and his son didn't have the chance "to fight that battle together." I wanted to tell Bruce that staying to fight the fire with your teenage son isn't all it's cracked up to be.

Thanks to Bruce, Tanesha, and the probation department staff, the youth were safe. Not so the staff. While the youth wore masks and remained on the bus, the staff had run around without protection to save Campus Kilpatrick from burning down. Many had to go to the hospital afterwards for smoke inhalation. Some had to go on disability. Others needed counseling. It's fair to wonder why the department's leadership hadn't ordered the youth evacuated the night before. Not only were there two fires burning nearby but the deputized staff weren't even sleeping at the facility due to the bed bug infestation. Clearly, the folks in charge, based over fifty miles away in Downey, had underestimated the fire leaving those at Campus Kilpatrick in a life-or-death situation.

Ten days after the fire, Tanesha got married. Her father, a pastor, performed the ceremony. He was just happy he wasn't giving her eulogy.

Bruce took three months off to "regroup," using every vacation day he had as well as all the sick time he'd accumulated in his twenty years. He could've filed for disability but felt that those who'd stayed at Campus Kilpatrick were the ones truly affected by the fire.

The kids credited the staff with saving their lives—and the facility.

Unfortunately, Campus Kilpatrick didn't remain saved, though it wasn't a stray ember on day two or three that got it but mudslides from the heavy rains that followed the fire. The probation department's brand-new flagship location was damaged so badly that it had to be closed.

Mullen's decision to stop the staff and youth from evacuating at the last second likely saved lives and prevented serious injury. Two of the deaths in the Woolsey Fire happened when a mother and son hadn't evacuated early enough and were burned alive in their car. His decision to shelter in place proved to be the right one. But it was another decision to shelter in place on a far larger scale that became one of the most contentious issues to arise from the Woolsey Fire.

And this time it wasn't forty some people at risk but 3,000 students at nearby Pepperdine University.

Bruce's mom holding the St. Bernard bank that also survived the 1906 San Francisco Fire.

PHOTO LORI BATES-TEMKIN

Pepperdine students waiting in the cafeteria as the Woolsey Fire approached.
PHOTO MADELEINE CARR

9

SHELTER IN PLACE

Pepperdine University sits smack dab in the middle of Malibu, practically a divider between the western and eastern parts of the city. Its campus was originally in south central Los Angeles, but a donation of 138 ocean-view acres in 1968 brought the university to the beach. The gift came from descendants of Frederick and May Rindge, the original owners of Rancho Malibu. The campus was officially opened in September of 1972 with a class of fewer than 1,000 students. Today, the university has over 3,000.

Madeleine Carr was a junior at the university and the news editor of the *Pepperdine Graphic*, the student run news organization. On the evening of Wednesday, November 7, she was supposed to go to the Borderline Bar in nearby Thousand Oaks with fellow students. When she received a text later that night about a mass shooting there, she told me she felt "a pit in her stomach."

She rushed to the newsroom where the staff had gathered, along with their faculty advisor, Dr. Elizabeth Smith. Madeleine spent the night there, constantly refreshing over eighty different websites on her computer searching for any information on the students who'd gone to the Borderline, including a *Graphic* editor.

As the hours wore on, only one student remained unaccounted for.

Alaina Housley was a freshman and something rare at Pepperdine—a double legacy. Her mother and father had both attended the school and met there. Alaina's Uncle, Adam Housley, played baseball on Pepperdine's 1992 National Championship team and later for the major leagues. Adam's wife, actress Tamera Mowry-Housley, also attended the university. To have so many connections at a relatively young school was almost unprecedented.

Madeleine knew Alaina since they both lived in DeBell House, a freshmen dormitory. Although Madeleine was a junior, she was permitted to live there because her roommate and best friend, Jenna, was the dorm's spiritual living advisor. As a school with a Christian mission, Pepperdine created the position, which differed from the dorm's resident advisor roles, to provide emotional support for students. This often included reading passages from the *Bible*.

Madeleine had interviewed Alaina twice for articles in the *Graphic*. One of the pieces was about Waves Weekend, the annual event for alumni and families of current students. Madeleine chose to interview Alaina because she'd attended many Waves Weekends with her parents but this would be her first as a student. That interview was a month before the shooting.

When there was no word on Alaina by 5:00 a.m., Madeleine began to lose hope. At 9:00 a.m., Dr. Smith asked her to draft an announcement about Alaina's passing. Madeleine read the piece over a hundred times, hoping and praying it would never be posted.

Curt Portzel is Pepperdine's executive director for estate and gift planning. If he'd been around in 1968, he would've handled the donation from the Rindge descendants. Portzel is also an alumnus of the university, earning a Bachelor of Arts degree in 1992.

On the morning of Thursday, November 8, Portzel was up at 5:00 a.m. As he put on his suit and tie for work, his phone exploded with texts and voicemails from friends and relatives on the East Coast about a shooting at the Borderline Bar.

As Portzel scoured the Internet for information, he saw that Adam Housley had posted "pray for my niece." Portzel quickly learned that Alaina Housley was a freshman at Pepperdine—and that she was missing. Hours after the shooting, the young woman's phone was still showing up as lying on the Borderline's dance floor.

Portzel rushed from his Westlake Village home to campus where the mood was somber. A prayer service was called for 11:00 a.m. Minutes before Pepperdine's president, Andrew Benton, was due to address the school, Alaina's uncle and aunt posted that their niece was one of the twelve people killed at the Borderline.

As tears flowed in the newsroom, Madeleine posted the notice of Alaina's death. Some of the staff went to the ceremony, others watched as it live streamed in the newsroom. Madeleine was worried about her roommate since it was Jenna's job to support the students in Alaina's dorm. Madeline wondered who would support Jenna.

When she arrived at DeBell House, it was "super quiet," unusual for a dorm full of eighteen-year-old women. She described the scene as "eerie" and "heavy." She found Jenna and hugged her for five minutes straight. But she also realized nothing she could do there would help. While she lived in DeBell, Madeleine was the only non-freshman in the dorm besides Jenna and the resident advisors. She didn't know the younger girls that well and felt out of place so she headed back to the newsroom.

"You're doing too much. You need to get some sleep," Dr. Smith told her, concerned about Madeleine's emotional state.

"I can't sleep. I can't eat. I can't watch TV. I can't do anything, except refresh Twitter," Madeleine replied.

A good friend called and said her father wanted to take them out to lunch to get them off campus and away from the grief that permeated every interaction.

"Do you think it's okay?" Madeleine asked Dr. Smith.

"You need a break. Go."

She met up with her friend and they drove over Malibu Canyon toward the San Fernando Valley. At lunch, she had a sandwich—her first meal in a while. She got a five-dollar cupcake. The lunch was supposed to be about decompressing but *NBC Nightly News* called wanting to interview her.

She hurried back for an on-camera interview, which felt "weird" since the reporter wanted to know what Alaina was like. Madeleine didn't consider herself close enough to answer such questions, but she also wanted to protect Alaina's friends from having to do so.

After the interview, she returned to the newsroom, but it was like she'd stepped into a different day. When she'd left a few hours earlier, people were crying. Now they were anxiously discussing two fires.

"What fires?" Madeleine asked.

"Where have you been?" one of the editors asked her.

In the time she'd been gone, two fires had broken out in the areas surrounding the shooting. Smoke from the fires was visible from the Borderline where many had gone to pay to their respects.

That was how fast the day had changed.

Portzel let his staff leave early since many of them lived close to the fires. An hour later, he drove home. On the 101 Freeway, he could see smoke. When he arrived home, his community was already under voluntary evacuation. To be safe, he and his wife and son decided to spend the night with friends who lived on Pepperdine's campus. On the drive back to Malibu around 11:00 that evening, Portzel could see an orange glow from the flames. Thick clouds of smoke covered the roads, making it "like driving in heavy fog."

When he arrived, two other families had come from over the hill to stay with his friend so Portzel and his dog slept in the car. Around six the next morning, Portzel got up thinking he and his family might head into Santa Monica for the day since Pepperdine had cancelled classes. That's when he received a call from his boss, Keith Hinkle, Pepperdine's senior vice-president for advancement and public affairs.

"I'm in Portland," Hinkle said, "You're my backup."

"For what?" Portzel asked.

"The Pepperdine EOC. The fire has crossed the 101. It's coming your way."

Portzel vaguely remembered that he was part of the Emergency Operations Center. The shirt the university had given him to wear in the case of an emergency still had the tag on it.

"You need to report ASAP to TAC."

The Thornton Administrative Center is one of the main buildings on Pepperdine's campus. As Portzel prepared to head there, his wife and son evacuated to Santa Monica.

At 7:07 a.m., the university gave the order for its students to shelter in place. Since 1993, shelter in place had been Pepperdine's policy, despite the fact that numerous wildfires had either burned the campus or come extremely close. In the 1985 Piuma Fire, flames burned within thirty yards of buildings, forcing students to flee their dormitories. The policy had been developed in conjunction with the LA County Fire Department, which believed that sheltering in place was a viable option in certain situations.

Because of the school's Mediterranean-style architecture, the roofs were ceramic tile and the walls were stucco, both good fire deterrents. President Benton believed the buildings were built to withstand fire. The university prided itself on its brush clearance. Its large grass lawn was regularly cut to the ground. Portzel thought it ugly and wished they would let it grow out a bit. He understood why, however, having gone through previous fires. The greenness played a role in preventing the spread of fires and was enhanced by two water reclamation ponds, which contained eight million gallons in total.

Pepperdine built the ponds to recycle water, but they were often used by LA County Firehawk helicopters during fire events.

At approximately the same time Pepperdine was telling its staff and student body to shelter in place, the local fire and sheriff departments were ordering the entire city of Malibu (and numerous other areas) to evacuate. In an abundance of caution, and without regard for the gridlock that decision would create on the Pacific Coast Highway, they called for a mandatory evacuation.

By the time Portzel made it to the EOC, all of the senior administrators were already there, from President Benton to various deans to VPs like him. Televisions had been set up to follow the fire on the news. Students were ordered to head to either the cafeteria or the gym. While the total student body numbered approximately 3,000, Portzel said there were no more than 800 students in the two locations. Despite what the university claimed about students not having cars, the vast majority of them had already evacuated, most in their own vehicles.

Madeleine didn't know what happened if a fire came close to campus, but she packed a go bag and went with the rest of her dorm to the cafeteria where all of the freshmen and most sophomores went. As a junior, Madeleine's friends were in the gym with the seniors. The cafeteria was "super crowded" with students but also with faculty, children, and pets. Disposable N95 masks were handed out to protect the students from breathing in the hazardous particles in the air, but few students wore them.

Someone brought their chinchilla.

As Friday morning moved into the afternoon, the numbers in the cafeteria began to go down as more students evacuated on their own. At 1:00 p.m., the shelter in place order was lifted as the winds had shifted, though the students were warned they might have to come back. Madeleine was busy writing news stories on her computer so she stayed in the cafeteria. She sent Jenna to their room for the five-dollar cupcake.

An hour later, Pepperdine told the students to shelter in place again.

When the students returned, there were far fewer of them—though they had a lot more stuff. Madeleine's parents called in a state of panic. They didn't understand why she was still on campus and directly in the path of a major wildfire.

"I'll pay for a hotel," her father said, as if cost was the reason she hadn't left.

"I'd go if I could get out," she said, sure the PCH was still gridlocked as it had been all morning. But by three o'clock in the afternoon, the ride into Santa Monica would take no longer than it would on a day of normal summer beach traffic. I know because that's when I drove down the PCH.

Someone started playing Disney songs on the piano in the cafeteria. The students began an impromptu sing along to "Go the Distance" from *Hercules*. Later, the cafeteria reverberated with the sounds of "Bohemian Rhapsody" and "Don't Stop Believin'."

By 5:00 p.m., Madeleine noticed the air quality in the cafeteria was getting worse. For a brief moment, she thought someone was grilling barbeque. She went outside to video chat with her mother and showed her how red the landscape was.

"That's not the sunset," Madeleine explained.

"You get inside right now," said her mother.

But the air kept getting worse as people were going in and out to check on the fire's progress. The students were ordered to wear their N95 masks, even when inside.

———

Portzel and the Pepperdine staff spent the day keeping the students in both the cafeteria and gym fed, and managing the situation while clouds of black smoke grew larger—and came closer. Portzel found it odd that there weren't more firefighters on campus. In past fires, the fire department used Pepperdine's large parking areas as a hub. In return, the university fed the firefighters and opened its dormitories for them to take a nap or have a shower.

Around eight o'clock that evening, five sheriffs' vehicles roared through the campus, lights blazing. Portzel and other EOC members rushed outside, but the sheriffs only needed to use Pepperdine's bathrooms. Relieved it was a false alarm, Portzel went back inside. The students in the gym were moved to the library since that building was closer to the cafeteria. Portzel estimated there were now fewer than 600 students present in both locations.

An hour or so later, a larger group of sheriffs' vehicles came flying onto the campus, again with their lights blazing. Portzel figured word about the clean bathrooms had gotten out. But instead, the sheriffs entered the cafeteria building shouting, "What are you doing here? You need to evacuate. The fire's coming!"

Madeleine prepared to follow their orders, leaving anything she couldn't run with, including her ukulele. Dr. Smith had two small children, who were sleeping on the cafeteria floor in a makeshift tent. Madeleine got the kids ready while trying not to scare the hell out of them.

But then senior Pepperdine administrators came into the building.

"No, no, no, we are not running. It's going to be okay," one of them said.

They huddled with the sheriffs, who'd been receiving calls from panicked parents begging them to evacuate their children. A few tense minutes later, the sheriffs left.

"When people get into a big hurry—fire department, sheriff's department—their instinct is to get everybody out of harm's way and move them, move them, move them," Benton told students in an effort to calm them, words that were captured on video and posted on social media. "The question is, where do you go? How do you get there? We don't think that's best."

The fire hit Pepperdine shortly thereafter at approximately eleven o'clock that night. There were flames on both sides of the campus. The wind was howling. Three Firehawk helicopters made nonstop drops to prevent the fire from burning down the campus and also to stop it from going into the adjacent development, Malibu Country Estates. If the fire were to jump the Pepperdine campus, it could charge all the way into eastern Malibu, perhaps even Topanga and then Santa Monica.

"Is this how the world ends?" Portzel thought.

Inside the cafeteria and library the kids were hot. And scared. Madeleine described a "weird upset" in the room after everyone was yelled at by the sheriffs. It was loud too. Firehawk helicopters buzzed over the building like angry hornets.

Portzel said there were only two fire engines on the campus, when in the past, there had been many more. To him, the firefighters seemed to "be on defense" the entire time. No one was taking any showers this time around.

Just before four o'clock in the morning, the firestorm passed and Portzel went outside. He could see that the fire had ripped directly through the campus. Char marks were visible on trees. Windows had warped from the heat. Cars were melted. Sheds and outbuildings had been destroyed. But the campus had, for the most part, survived. As had all of its students.

When the school finally released the shelter in place order at 8:00 a.m., Madeleine's throat was killing her. She first thought she had strep, like any normal kid would, but then realized that she was suffering from smoke inhalation. The school reminded the students to always wear their masks.

When she went outside to get a mini-bus back to her dorm, the campus looked like the desert planet Tatooine in *Star Wars*. Madeleine wasn't sure if she needed to wear her mask in the shower too and decided it would be safer to evacuate to her friend's home in Santa Barbara.

She'd had quite enough of sheltering in place.

In the days that followed, many Malibuites wondered why Pepperdine students didn't evacuate since—despite arguments to the contrary—plenty of time existed to do so. The university issued its call to shelter in place Friday morning at 7:07 a.m. but flames didn't arrive on campus until 10:45 p.m. Pepperdine had sixteen hours to evacuate approximately 600 students. By the afternoon, the PCH wasn't even jammed anymore. Buses could have easily made it onto the campus, loaded the students, and driven them to Santa Monica *hours* before flames made it to Pepperdine.

Malibuites wondered if the resources spent protecting the students could have been used to save some of the nearly 1,000 homes lost. Most Malibu neighborhoods saw no helicopters, yet Pepperdine had three making drops continuously for hours. There were also rumors of dozens of engines leaving other areas in Malibu to fight the fire on the Pepperdine campus, rumors I was unable to confirm.

Some wondered if the decision to have students stay was designed to ensure the survival of Pepperdine's campus. Certainly, without the hundreds of water drops, the campus would have been overrun with flames, as it was in a 1970 fire just before the university was built. That fire scorched every inch of the property. Without the water drops, the campus would have suffered significantly more damage. No matter how fire resistant, buildings burn given enough time and heat. Was it possible that, in their desire to save their school, Pepperdine leaders had used their students as human shields?

This is number ten of an unknown number of Pepperdine buses.

PHOTO ROBERT KERBECK

This is the destroyed greenhouse of Zuma Canyon Orchids.
PHOTO ROBERT KERBECK

10

I WILL DIE IN ORCHIDS

Nestled into the base of Zuma Canyon, a mere third of a mile from the busy Pacific Coast Highway, is an unusual concentration of a flower not native to Southern California—the orchid. A local treasure, Zuma Canyon Orchids has been the Vazquez family business for over half a century since Amado Vazquez, a charter member of the Malibu Orchid Society, purchased Arthur Freed Orchids in 1978. Amado had been the head grower at Arthur Freed, and he quickly renamed and moved the business to its current location.

Under the obsessive care of Amado, his wife, Maria, and their son, George, Zuma Canyon Orchids went on to win more than 600 awards and certificates, including the Royal Horticultural Society's Westonbirt Gold Medal for outstanding achievement in orchids. Over the years, regular clients have included Frank and Nancy Sinatra, Robert Wagner and Natalie Wood, Sting, Michael Crichton, Heidi Klum, Julia Louis-Dreyfus, and many other A-list celebrities. In 1994, the International Phalaenopsis Alliance bestowed its lifetime achievement award on Amado, who was then in his late seventies and still working hard. Through the family's efforts, Zuma Canyon Orchids became something precious and unique to the Malibu area—and Amado himself became a local legend.

An ambitious floriculturist who emigrated to California from Mexico in the late 1940s, Amado had a way of tricking young people into loving orchids as much as he did. With his receding hairline, neat mustache, and easy smile, Amado would give visiting children a tour of his greenhouses and then for a finale, he'd gift them a flower.

"Let's see if they might be an orchid person," he'd say after they'd delightedly gone on their way.

It was both an act of generosity and a shrewd business decision. Amado was a Mexican immigrant starting a new venture. He needed customers, and this was a smart way to get them hooked early. Often, this first free orchid encouraged the person to become a lifelong customer. More than that, Amado's free-orchid policy inadvertently planted the seeds of his future stature in a way he could never have imagined.

In the early 1950s, while she was an undergrad at Berkeley, writer and journalist Joan Didion came to see Amado's orchids for the first time when she was home visiting her parents, who lived in Malibu. Amado gave Didion an orchid, but just as importantly he allowed her to meander in the greenhouses, something she loved to do. "All my life I've been trying to spend time in one greenhouse or another," she wrote in "Quiet Days in Malibu," the final essay of her classic 1979 book, *The White Album*. Didion often took her lunch at Arthur Freed Orchids since she "craved the particular light and silence of greenhouses," and she appreciated Amado's devotion to the flowers. Standing together in an extravagant sea of them, Amado told her, "I will die in orchids."

Didion wrote of something else at the end of *The White Album*: wildfire.

In the penultimate essay of the book, "On the Morning After the Sixties," she describes in stark, violent prose how the 1978 Kanan Fire burned 25,000 acres in and around Malibu, destroyed nearly 500 homes and structures, and killed three people. The blaze also burned down the greenhouses she'd treated as a second home, taking 15,000 of Amado's beloved orchids with it. When Didion came and saw the destruction, the loss nearly caused the famously dispassionate author to break down in tears. Amado had lost years of work. But his focus was already on re-growing his orchids and rebuilding his business.

"I started with nothing," Amado told his son George the day after the Kanan Fire. He grabbed a wheelbarrow and a shovel, and the two of them began cleaning up. Competitors gave the Vazquez family orchids to help them rebreed their stock. Despite having no income for more than a year, Amado continued to pay his workers. And eventually, under his dogged, delicate touch, Zuma Canyon Orchids bloomed anew.

In 1985, George took over Zuma Canyon Orchids, though his father continued to work until he died in 2013. Like many who grew up in Malibu, George loved to surf and as a kid in the '50s and the '60s, he did whatever he could to spend time in the waves at nearby Zuma Beach. Amado agreed to let George surf as often and for as long as he liked, provided he help out at Freed's, which young George called the "Orchid Ranch." By making George put his hands in the soil at a young age, Amado encouraged his son to fall in love with the flowers.

Years later, George was so successful in the family business that he received an invitation to dine at Kensington Palace with Princess Margaret. Before she presented him with the Royal Horticultural Society's Westonbirt Gold Medal, George was instructed how to bow and told not to shake hands with the princess. When the moment came, he impulsively extended his hand and to his surprise she shook it. To make up for the *faux pas*, he—naturally—sent her a dozen of his best orchids.

George was twenty-seven years old at the time of the 1978 fire. Almost exactly forty years later, on the day of the Woolsey Fire, he was nine days away from closing escrow on selling Zuma Canyon Orchids to a customer he'd had for decades. The deal was a classic handshake agreement, sealed over lunch without realtors. The buyer wanted to give the business to his stepdaughter, who planned to retain George's staff and continue providing his lifelong customers with the orchids they loved. It seemed the perfect way to pass on the business.

Though his heart would always be in orchids, and he would retain his position as an American Orchid Society Emeritus Judge, it had become time to move on. He and his wife of thirty-eight years, Bonnie, were ready to retire. Their three kids lived in northern California, and George and Bonnie wanted to be closer to them. Their oldest son is a teacher, their middle son a renowned chef. Their daughter, Sierra, had worked at Zuma Canyon Orchids and displayed great acumen for the business but she fell in love with a man from the Napa area and left LA too. By October 2018, George and Bonnie had sold their southern California home and were living peacefully in Solano County just east of Napa Valley.

At noon on Friday, November 9, not quite twenty-four hours after the fire had been reported, George received a call from his head grower, Oli Alvarado.

"The fire is coming," he said. "What should I do?"

Oli and his wife, Ana, who was the office manager, had worked at Zuma Canyon Orchids for more thirty-five years. Like George, they had a life-spanning attachment to it.

"Get the workers out and leave," said George. He knew most of his workers lived in Oxnard, a half-hour north, and he didn't want them trapped in Malibu if the PCH was shut down. "Get out before they close the highway."

"What should I take?" asked Oli.

"Just the computers."

A long silence played over the line.

Inside the greenhouses were more than 15,000 orchids, the same number that had burned in the '78 fire. Those flowers were worth millions of dollars, but they represented more than money. In a world where orchids are now sold at supermarkets, Zuma Canyon Orchids had survived (and thrived) by creating something that set them apart: living works of art.

In lieu of using wooden stakes to hold up the fragile plants, George's staff used wire that they matched to the color of each stem so to keep it hidden.

"Something has to hold the orchid from falling over," George later told me, "but that doesn't mean you have to see it."

To wrap the wire to the stem, they imported colored tape from Japan that was carefully matched to the shade of the blossom. Rather than plant their orchids in clay or plastic pots, Zuma Canyon Orchids nestled them in antique Japanese wooden boxes or Chinese porcelain pots or whatever the client wanted. They arranged plants together in the shape of a heart or to make a waterfall effect. Over the decades, Amado and George had even created new hybrids for customers. For instance, socialite heiress and style icon Betsy Bloomingdale asked them to name an orchid after the First Lady and so in 1982, Phalaenopsis Nancy Reagan was born.

"The computers? That's it?" Oli asked, seeming to need confirmation that everything should be left behind, even the impressive collection of books on orchids, some more than 150 years old, that George had amassed inside the greenhouse.

"That's it," said George, his voice heavy with sadness and resolve.

If he'd been living in the area, he would have stayed to fight the fire, but he wasn't going to put his staff in jeopardy. As much as he loved his orchids, he loved his people more.

The caretaker of the home next door to Zuma Canyon Orchids was Alfonso Fuentes, a well-tanned bulldog of a man. In his early fifties, he had jet-black hair and a mustache, both peppered with gray. He'd worked in Malibu since moving from Oaxaca, Mexico in 1986. His first place of employment in the United States was in Trancas Canyon just north of Zuma Beach.

The home where Alfonso now worked had recently been purchased by Cornelia Funke, author of the popular young-adult fantasy series *Inkheart.* Funke was working with Oscar-winning filmmaker Guillermo del Toro on a book adaption of his 2007 film *Pan's Labyrinth*, and she had tasked Alfonso, whom she nicknamed "El Brujo" (the Warlock), with transforming her new property into something as magical as a setting from one of her books. Alfonso cleared years of overgrown brush to make pathways that snaked up the hillside and carved out "outdoor rooms" tucked off the trails. At the top, he built a corral along with a spot for a trailer that would be lodging for a writer-in-residence program Cornelia wanted to launch.

On the morning of November 9, Alfonso and his crew—Roberto, Sixto, Ronnie, and Jamie—arrived at Funke's home at seven o'clock to meet two men who were delivering large trees.

Funke had heard the reports of the approaching wildfire, but she is German and had no experience with them.

"What should I do?" she asked. "Do you think I should leave?"

"Let's wait," said Alfonso, who did have experience with Malibu fires. "Someone's gonna come to help."

He recalled that within minutes of the start of the December 2017 fire that burned above my street in Malibu Park, firefighters arrived on the scene and a Firehawk helicopter dropped water on the flames. That fire was smothered before it had a chance to spread.

But at nine o'clock, as the smoke in the Zuma Canyon hills became noticeably thicker, it wasn't the fire department that showed up but sheriffs shouting on bullhorns, "Evacuate! Evacuate!"

Funke left immediately, but Alfonso and his crew wanted to wet down her property first. As soon as they were finished, the men rushed to his truck, and the two men delivering the trees followed Alfonso down Bonsall Drive and out of the neighborhood. When they got to the PCH, however, it was backed up down the coast. Alfonso pulled off by the Point Dume Plaza Shopping Center on Heathercliff Road and offered to buy his men and the tree guys lunch at Lily's, which is known for having some of the best food in Malibu. The line to order often stretched outside the door but today the restaurant was closed. So was the Pavilions market next door.

When Alfonso turned to view the Santa Monica Mountains in the distance to the north, he understood why. The shopping center sat on a hilltop that provided a panoramic view of the mountains on the opposite side of the highway.

He could see most of Zuma Canyon—and the flames tearing at the tops of the ridges.

He found Lily there at the end of the lot watching the fire. "They ordered me to close because of the danger," she said.

"I left behind two burros," Alfonso said, regretting out loud that he hadn't thought to evacuate Funke's two donkeys, El Zorro and Esperanza. Like others who left animals behind, he hadn't realized the severity of the situation soon enough. "One of them is pregnant."

Lily seemed stricken by the news. She'd recently lost her daughter to cancer, and the thought of inflicting more sorrow on her was more than Alfonso could bear.

I gotta save those burros.

Leaving Jamie to guard his truck, Alfonso and the other men took off on foot down the shoulder of the PCH. He knew the sheriffs were now blocking access to the Bonsall neighborhood so they hopped fences to follow old dirt trails. When they reemerged onto Bonsall, Alfonso spotted a neighbor who had a horse trailer and told him why he'd returned.

"I've got room for one animal," the man said.

But Esperanza and El Zorro were a couple and they were expecting. Certainly, one or both of the animals would react badly to being separated.

"No," Alfonso said, "They need to stay together."

He and the men pushed on to Funke's property and saw that the fire had come much closer. Up the street, homes were ablaze. They quickly wet the house and grounds again, then led the burros to a corral at a home down Bonsall Canyon that was further from the flames. Then, though no one had asked them to, the men decided to go back and fight the fire.

Funke's neighbors, Larry and Laurel Thorne, owned the Thorne Family Farm and sold their organic fruits and produce to local markets and restaurants. For years, they had been running a farming camp to teach children about growing, sustainability, and animal husbandry. My son attended that camp for two summers when he was a boy.

Alfonso had worked with the Thornes for more than thirty years. He worried that the fire would destroy their farm and its acres of produce, which sat on the other side of Funke's property from Zuma Canyon Orchids. Alongside the Thornes, who had decided to stay, Alfonso and his men fought for hours to save both properties. When the nearby hydrant went dry, the men slapped at the fire with tree branches, which often caught fire and had to be extinguished or discarded. Sprinting from one spot fire to another, they banged and banged until their arms felt like melted rubber—and until the fires, by some miracle, were out. Heaving from the effort and bathed in sweat, Alfonso realized they hadn't seen a single firefighter.

It was 5:00 p.m. and the firestorm had passed through. Somehow, they'd kept both properties safe. Alfonso could see that just up the road the Orchid Ranch was also still standing. He'd been keeping his eye on the Vazquez property as well.

We saved them. It's over.

After the briefest of respites, Alfonso and his crew went to help other neighbors whose homes were in jeopardy. An hour had passed when Alfonso spotted something that sent a shiver down his spine despite the heat of the fire all around him: an angry explosion of orange at Zuma Canyon Orchids.

A storage shed had caught fire, most likely from a stray ember. As Alfonso and his men rushed to contain it, the blaze leapt to the greenhouses. They did the best they could but the fire was too powerful. It tore at the wood frame of the greenhouses and poured down into the flowers' sanctuary. As the men watched, frustrated and grim, the orchids were devoured, one by one, row by row.

Not one survived. When it was over, not a single bloom remained. In a perverse irony, the only thing left untouched was a large white sign dangling from the destroyed roof that read, *No Smoking in Greenhouse.*

Alfonso knew he had to call George Vazquez, a man he'd known for more than thirty years. He'd known George's father, Amado, as well. It was the kind of call no one wanted to make.

"I'm sorry," Alfonso said, trying to summon up the words. "I tried. But I couldn't save the greenhouse."

George skipped past the loss of his orchids. "Are you okay?" he asked. "Are you injured?"

"I tried to save it."

"I know. Are your guys okay?"

"Yes. I'm so sorry."

"Thank you, Alfonso. Thank you for trying."

Forty years after the Kanan Fire had destroyed his father's orchids and nine days from selling the business, George had lost everything.

———

Five months later, my friend, Tommy, and I rode our bikes to visit the remains of George's Orchid Ranch. George had continued to pay his staff and was close to "stopping the bleeding" by settling with his insurance company, though he doubted he'd receive enough money to rebuild. He wasn't the only one. Many residents, especially elderly ones, had too little coverage. Most individuals didn't have something called "building code upgrade insurance"—or the money in the bank to pay for those additional costs. The city of Malibu too was insisting on enforcing codes that hadn't existed when Amado built the greenhouses. As a result, a large percentage of homeowners could be forced to sell.

When we arrived, the gate to Zuma Canyon Orchids was locked, and as we stood outside, a man in a pickup truck pulled up. Because Tommy had rented the property next door before Cornelia Funke bought it, he recognized Oli Alvarado, George's head grower. Oli let us in to wander the remains of the grounds, much like I imagined Joan Didion had forty years earlier when the Kanan Fire destroyed Amado's orchids.

Tommy was more interested in seeing what Alfonso had done to Cornelia's property and hiked up the hillside to peer over the fence that separated the properties. As it turned out, Alfonso had managed to save El Zorro and

Esperanza, but their baby foal died shortly after birth from the effects of the smoke, yet another victim of the blaze.

I turned toward the wreckage of the greenhouses. Like so many properties in Malibu, Zuma Canyon Orchids still hadn't been cleared of debris, and as I walked I felt the crunch of shattered glass that had once been in the ceiling of the greenhouse.

Under what remained of the building's twisted frame, a series of wooden benches had collapsed or been reduced to ash, though a few were intact. Atop those still standing were the scorched remains of the orchids.

I suddenly understood why Didion had welled up in tears at the sight. Thousands of blackened stems curled up toward burned blossoms, their myriad tints and shades replaced by ash gray. Among the casualties were unique colors bred by Amado and George, varieties that didn't exist elsewhere. After the '78 fire, Amado asked Didion if he could breed an orchid and name it after her. She of course said yes, and he asked what color she wanted it to be. Thus was born Phalaenopsis Joan Didion Dunne, pink with a light rose striping and a red lip. I recently asked George how he would describe the orchid, now gone, and he said, "Emotional." When I pressed him to be more specific about what feeling Didion's orchid provoked, he didn't hesitate. "Hope."

Before Tommy and I left, I wanted to thank Oli for letting us in and giving me a chance to grieve. In my search for him, I knocked on the door of one of the remaining structures, then opened it. No one was inside, but I discovered there what George had been talking about. The small, shed-like building had been converted into a makeshift mini-greenhouse. Several wooden tables had been pushed together in the cramped space. And there, in that particular light and silence, stood two rows of orchids, their stems erect and defiant in glorious white-yellow-pink-purple bloom.

Zuma Canyon Orchids was starting over, again.

New life at Zuma Canyon Orchids

PHOTO ROBERT KERBECK

The skies above Paradise Cove Pier filled with clouds of toxic smoke and ash.

PHOTO SIMEON STURGES

11

PARADISE SAVED

Simeon and Ryder Sturges were another father-and-son team that fought the Woolsey Fire. Unlike me and my son, however, these two knew what they were doing. Simeon's grandfather had been the fire chief of Santa Monica. Twenty-year-old Ryder wanted to follow in his great-grandfather's footsteps and is studying fire technology at Oxnard College.

The two live near the beach in the Paradise Cove Mobile Home Park, the setting of the 1970s TV series, *The Rockford Files*. Both men had spent their entire lives in the community of 271 trailer homes and knew every inch of its property. Simeon's parents had bought their single-wide for $9,000 in 1977.

Simeon's first memory of fire was in 1978 when he saw flames from his bedroom window. And in 1982, when he was ten, he was out on a boat with his grandfather when they learned of a fire in the Cove. Simeon imagined losing his most prized possession, a collection of baseball cards. When they returned to land, they watched the news and saw that a dozen or so homes had burned. While theirs was not one of them, these childhood experiences created a fire anxiety. Anytime Simeon saw smoke, he assumed a fire was coming his way.

On the day the Woolsey Fire started, Ryder was shaken by the news of the shooting the night before at the Borderline Bar and Grill. He had friends who were supposed to go to the bar. That afternoon, he drove to Thousand Oaks to donate blood and waited in line for two hours. That's when he spotted smoke from the nearby fires. A lifelong surfer, Ryder was familiar with weather patterns. The Santa Ana winds were blowing hard and predicted to increase.

Oh crap. That fire's gonna reach Malibu.

When he got up Friday morning, his mother Julie told him to pack. Ryder loaded his most prized possessions into his truck: fifteen surfboards and a wetsuit.

"Really, that's where your priorities are?" Julie said when she saw he'd packed no clothes, let alone sentimental items or pictures.

"Yup."

At 11:30 a.m., Ryder climbed onto the roof of their trailer and saw flames on the hillsides above Paradise Cove. People were streaming into the parking lot, fleeing from neighborhoods on the land side of the PCH, which were already on fire. Because the Paradise Cove Beach Café had a generator, the parking lot became a make-shift evacuation center. Or as Simeon described it, "a shit show." Horses ran loose. People were in hysterics. One man, Josh Gabbard, had fled from Malibu Park after he was hit in the head by a roofing tile. He appeared to be in shock from the firenado which ripped through the neighborhood, tearing off roofs and tipping over trucks.

Simeon made the rounds of the Cove, checking to be sure that every trailer had a connected garden hose. He shut off each trailer's propane tanks too. A few hours later, smoke pouring down the hillside made it seem as if it were already nighttime. By 3:00 p.m., the fire was threatening to jump the PCH, and people began to evacuate from the Cove. Ryder kept thinking he'd see a bunch of fire engines on the highway but there weren't any.

Around six o'clock, the fire jumped the highway.

Simeon and Ryder hosed down their roof, but the fire was going to hit other homes closer to the highway before theirs. Because most of the trailers were feet apart, if one went up in flames, the whole community would be in jeopardy. Already, the fire had burned the Seminole Springs Mobile Home Park in Agoura. Over one hundred homes had been completely melted.

"We need to go to the top of the cove and save those houses," said Ryder, determined not to lose the only home he'd ever known.

Just then, two LA County lifeguards pulled up in a utility vehicle called a Mule with 500 feet of fire hose in the back. An off-duty Santa Barbara firefighter was in the Cove helping his parents. He had a nozzle and a hydrant wrench. Simeon, Ryder, and a group of nine or ten men drove up to the PCH to fight the fire. When they reached the highway, there were a few spot fires on the ocean side, but on the land side, flames engulfed the entire hillside. Ryder thought they were "screwed." He figured they would do what they could until the fire department showed up.

The group laid out the hose and hooked it to the hydrant on the ocean side of the highway. The four-inch hose was heavy even without water, but once it was filled it required Ryder and six or seven others just to move it around. Simeon manned the nozzle and blasted the flames on the ocean side, putting most of them out. The men then focused on knocking down the fire on the land side. As they did, at least twenty engines drove past. Occasionally, they ran over the hoses in the middle of the highway but they never stopped. Finally, Ryder flagged one engine down. The captain in the passenger seat rolled down his window, flashed a thumbs up sign, and took off.

The message was clear. The group of men—and Paradise Cove—were on their own.

Simeon noticed that embers had crossed the highway and landed on the property of Laurene Powell, the widow of Steve Jobs. The $60 million estate was under construction and went from the PCH all the way to the ocean, yet no one was protecting it. The men couldn't get their hose through her locked driveway gate so they kicked it open.

Simeon's interest wasn't entirely altruistic. With the wind direction, embers from Powell's property were flying toward Paradise Cove. Already, a huge palm tree on her property was lit up like a sparkler. Still it was someone's home—even if it belonged to one of the richest women in the world. If he could do something to save it, he was going to try. Simeon caught sight of his wife evacuating just as he and Ryder disappeared behind a wall of flames on the Powell estate.

They tried to put out the palm tree but it was too tall. Their hose didn't have enough pressure to shoot that high. Two massive forty-foot tall construction tents full of tools and equipment exploded into flames behind them. A line of thirty flammable trees began to catch as well.

"We gotta bail. This property's too big," called Ryder.

But Simeon kept blasting the fire, which seemed everywhere, as the winds swirled around them. Neither man had any protective equipment, not even masks. Ryder wore a Black Sabbath 1978 World Tour T-shirt.

"Fuck these people," Ryder yelled, when his father wouldn't give up. "Dad, we have to save *our* house."

Reluctantly, Simeon loaded the hose into the Mule and the men drove the quarter mile back down to the Cove. On the hillside above the mobile home park, a line of pine trees was being bombarded with embers from the Powell property. One giant palm tree was already on fire, shooting flames a hundred feet into the air.

If the trees caught, Simeon feared the homes in the lower cove would burn. If the lower cove caught, embers from those homes would be driven toward another row of pine trees and the homes of the upper cove, as well as the community's rec center, which was made entirely of wood.

Ryder was on the roof of their mobile home, battling to hose off flaming embers before it was too late. At that moment, firefighters pulled into the cove looking for hydrants to fill their engine.

"Give us ten minutes," Simeon pleaded, exhausted from fighting the fire for eight hours straight. "Come on, you gotta do something. Do me a favor and put out that palm tree." He needed the break, emotionally and physically. He just wanted to "take a breath."

The firefighters didn't say anything. Simeon told me they didn't seem happy about lending a hand but they had little excuse. Simeon and Ryder already had their hose out, all the firefighters had to do was pick it up.

The firefighters put out the palm tree in two minutes, then filled their engines from the Cove's hydrants. As they pulled out, one of the firefighters shouted at Ryder, "Don't go on your roof."

Around midnight, an enormously tall and thick eucalyptus tree inside the community caught fire. Simeon and the men couldn't put it out on their own. To their relief, two engines on the highway stopped and began blasting the tree. Another engine drove into Paradise Cove to hit the tree from a different angle. Simeon wasn't sure why firefighters suddenly showed up to help the Cove but he was grateful. Perhaps because the fire front, the most dangerous part of the fire, had blown through to the ocean, the fire department decided it was now safe for them to attempt structure protection. The engines stayed for two hours until the fire was out.

Simeon and Ryder continued to put out hot spots into Saturday morning—often from their roof. Sometimes the fire snuck underground, going into one gopher hole and popping out at another. Finally, at 3:00 a.m., Ryder passed out.

But Simeon was afraid to go to sleep. He kept patrolling the cove, using a head lamp to find his way. At 4:30 a.m., he spotted flames in the same cul-de-sac that had burned in the '82 fire. Dried leaves between the highway and homes had ignited. Because Simeon had earlier attached garden hoses to each house, he could get water onto the fire before it spread. When he finished extinguishing the blaze, he wandered back to his house, practically begging the sun to come up and end his night of hell. Three times the cove had nearly burned and three times it was saved.

Ryder woke at six o'clock to find his father sleeping in a beach chair in the middle of the street, headlamp hanging over his face. In true father-son fashion, Ryder kicked the chair to wake him up. One of their neighbors, who'd been drinking more and more as the ordeal went on, stumbled out of his trailer. "You guys aren't doing anything," he shouted. "There's smoke right in front of you."

But it wasn't smoke, rather mist from pinholes in the fire hose, which was still full of water in case of a flare-up.

"If you don't stop panicking," Simeon said to the neighbor, "I'm gonna turn the hose on you."

As the sun came up and the sky rained ash, Simeon and Ryder realized their neighborhood had survived. Not one out of 271 homes had burned. Paradise Cove was the only neighborhood in western Malibu with zero losses.

While the immediate danger was over at Paradise Cove, Point Dume was still burning. Ryder ran into a group of friends that afternoon who lived on the Point.

"Get in the car," one of them shouted. "There's still so much fire."

Driving through the Dume neighborhood was "insane." Multiple houses were on fire but there were still no engines. Ryder's friends, who were mostly in their mid-twenties and early thirties, began putting out hot spots using shovels and dirt. At twenty, Ryder was the baby of the group. They nicknamed themselves the Point Dume Bombers since everyone in the group was a surfer who liked to surf big waves known as "bombs."

A former Marine, Robert Spangle, came up with a system to organize the group during the fire. Robert grew up in Malibu West and joined the military after graduating Malibu High in 2007. After serving two tours in Afghanistan, he returned to the area to live on Point Dume. A former reconnaissance Marine and radio specialist, he knew how to operate in "hostile territory." His role was to sneak behind enemy lines, gather information, and relay that intelligence. In Afghanistan, he had located snipers and established targets for air strikes. Commando raids were conducted based on what he'd learned. Lives depended on him being correct.

Robert wouldn't even have been in Malibu for the fire had he not crashed his motorcycle the day before. He and his former Marine team leader, John, were supposed to do a road trip to San Francisco that weekend. On his way into Venice to meet him on Thursday, Robert crashed his bike going sixty-five miles per hour. The only thing that saved him was the spare helmet he was carrying for John. When Robert was knocked off the bike, he slid the entire way *on that helmet.* Still, he had serious road rash on his legs. The skin on top of his right foot came off completely, but he was lucky to be alive—and not to have broken anything.

Since there would be no road trip, Robert headed back to Malibu and went to bed early to nurse his pain. When he woke up Friday, he could see smoke from his bedroom window.

Civilians, at best, prepare for *likely* scenarios. But in the military Robert had been taught to prepare for the *worst*. Limping around on his bad foot, Robert packed his car and parked it facing out. He filled barrels with water and hosed off the roof of the small house he was renting. His neighbor, Alan, was a tech guy who ordered everything online and didn't even have a car. Alan was complaining about being unable to get an Uber in order to evacuate. Robert promised to drive him into Santa Monica if the situation deteriorated.

Around 11:00 that morning, cell service went out. An *uh-oh* moment. Without power and cell service, Robert no longer had what the military terms "situational awareness." He decided it was time to go. Alan got into Robert's 1988 Mercedes convertible with a backpack full of hard drives and the two headed to Zuma Beach.

There things were descending into chaos. Lifeguards had cut open a chain-link fenced area to create a makeshift stall for horses, but one of the animals had stabbed its neck on a link and was now bleeding—and screaming. The air was practically unbreathable—and getting worse. Robert decided it was no longer safe there.

As he headed down the PCH toward Santa Monica, he spotted a fire on the land side of the highway. He pulled over and grabbed some emergency water from his car, dumping it on the flames. But the fire grew larger. He began scooping dirt onto the flames using the empty water container. Other citizens pulled over to help using their hands and feet to get dirt onto the fire. Finally, a man came down the hill with a front-loader. In minutes, he dumped enough dirt to put it out.

Robert dropped Alan off in Santa Monica and spent the night at his cousin's house there. Watching the news, he felt helpless as the fire continued to spread.

That night, he had trouble sleeping. Part of it was the pain from his legs, but he also felt awful he wasn't helping.

After leaving the Marines in 2011, Robert had studied fashion. During his apprenticeship on London's famed Savile Row, Robert had been steadily posting photos to his street style blog. An editor at *GQ* discovered them, and since then, his photography had been featured in some of the most prestigious magazines in the world, which meant he had a press pass—and access back into the fire zone. Determined to put the pass to good use, he returned the next morning.

He first went to his mother's home on Busch Drive but it was too late. The home was gone, along with everything inside it. He went back to Point Dume and found his own place was okay. He wanted to get a sense of where the fire was and how it was progressing, so he headed to the Point Dume headlands with his binoculars. From the tall vantage point of the headlands, he had a bird's eye view of most of the neighborhood. Right away, he spotted flames on Grasswood Avenue and headed over there. The smoke was so heavy he could barely see. When he arrived, he saw three white trucks and a large group of men wearing bandanas and masks: the Point Dume Bombers.

"Hey, I saw a fire over here," he said.

"We already took care of it," one of the men said.

Robert recognized some of the men from growing up in Malibu, but he didn't know any of them well. "Can I help you guys?"

For the remainder of Saturday, Robert fought fires side by side with the men until two in the morning. They all agreed to take a break for a few hours of sleep. When they met up at 4:30 that morning in the dark at the Pavilions shopping center, Robert floated an idea.

"If I took one of the walkie-talkies to the headlands," he said. "I could build an antenna to increase range and reception." The Bombers had been using three yellow kids' walkie-talkies to communicate but they barely worked.

"How are you going to do that?" Ryder asked.

"With some copper wire and a metal trash can lid, I can boost the signal. From the headlands I can spot fires and then relay the information via the walkie-talkies." Once, while stationed in Africa and "bored," Robert had used a hand-held radio and coat hangers to contact the International Space Station. Like many military types, he was too humble to brag about it.

"Where are you going to get copper wire?" someone else asked, practically with a snicker.

"I have some in my survival kit," he said, sounding a lot like MacGyver.

The Bombers looked at Robert like he was a kook and seemed to be reconsidering admitting him to their ranks.

"Wait, we should listen to this guy," said a Bomber who'd grown up in Malibu West and knew of Robert. "He was a reconnaissance Marine. He snuck behind enemy lines in Afghanistan. He can help us."

Convinced that Robert was the real deal, the Bombers split into two separate teams. Robert went to the headlands with a walkie-talkie, binoculars, copper wire, and a trash can lid. He wrapped the wire around the original rubber nub antenna of the walkie-talkie, sat it on the lid, and drew a map of the neighborhood's streets. He kept a log of events as they were happening. He'd radio whenever he spotted a flare-up and send one of the teams to the area. It seemed every time he was "spot on" about the location of the fire. He didn't leave his post for five days, sleeping under the stars, as he had in the Marines. From the moment he set up camp on Sunday morning, not a single home burned on Point Dume.

One night after finishing their rounds, Robert, Ryder, and the other men gathered at a home on Grasswood Avenue to listen to Waylon Jennings and drink Coors Light. A Bomber named Sam McGee had a tattoo gun hooked up to a generator and each man got a *PDB18* tattoo on his arm. It was the only time Robert left his post but he wanted to be part of the ceremony. He was impressed with the men, who he said were like a platoon of Marines. No one had showered or changed clothes for days. No one was getting any sleep. Yet no one complained.

For the next few days, the Bombers didn't have to worry about school or jobs or bills. It was like they weren't living in America anymore. Or maybe it was still America but the best version the country could be. The fire had brought the men—and the community—together. Someone needed food or water, you got it to them. A person wanted a generator, you found one and helped set it up. An elderly person needed medicine, you met a pharmacist at a checkpoint to get the prescription. All that mattered was helping others and saving something you loved more than yourself.

Your neighborhood.

The heat from the 2,000 degree flames melted the lettering on this Airstream.

PHOTO SIMEON STURGES

Supplies at the Point Dume Relief Center

PHOTO JUDY MERRICK

12

POINT DUME RELIEF CENTER

Judy Merrick looks like the Oscar-winning actress Allison Janney. She'd moved to Malibu from northern California in 2002, which meant I had her beat by two years. Malibuites measure themselves—and others—by how long they've lived in the city.

"I've been in Malibu for forty years," I heard a guy brag once at a party using that number to give him the upper hand in some argument.

"What's fifty get you?" was the response that came back.

The guy shut up.

Having both lived here just short of twenty years, Judy and I won't be bragging about our longevity in Malibu. Judy did have something, however, that gives her a leg up on me. She is married to one of those fifty-year locals, a realtor named Brian Merrick, the son of the legendary John Merrick, who'd been the municipal judge in Malibu for over twenty-five years. Judy and Brian live on Point Dume in the house he'd grown up in.

Throughout his childhood, Brian had seen many fires. His agreement with his mother was that he could watch—and fight—any fire so long as it didn't cross the PCH and enter their neighborhood. Then he would have to come home. But in his lifetime, no wildfire had ever burned into Point Dume and no one thought the Woolsey Fire would be the first. After all, no matter how big the fire, the firefighters had the firebreak of the PCH to stop it. Certainly, the highway would be lined with engines to ensure that homes remained safe.

But when flames crossed the highway and began to burn Point Dume in the late afternoon on Friday, November 9, there was no line of engines waiting to help. Many people had evacuated to homes on the Point from communities that already burned. My family had done so; like others, we believed we'd be safe there. We were wrong.

Brian began to prepare his property, filling trash cans with water and setting up wet towels to "snap" the fire out. That evening, they could hear the fire approaching "like a monster" as it devoured the wood of nearby homes, popping windows and exploding propane tanks. In her first fire, Judy was stamping out embers with her shoes. The fire came to the backside of their property, but they let it get no further. By Saturday at 2:00 a.m., after ten hours of flames, they felt as though they were out of harm's way. Sitting together at their kitchen table, they took a moment to savor that fact.

"You know I would never leave you," Brian said.

Judy was moved. Her husband wasn't normally an openly sentimental guy. "Thank you, honey," she said and touched his hand.

When Brian looked up at her, frowning, she knew. "You weren't talking to me, were you?" Judy asked.

"No," Brian admitted, "I was talking to the house."

Later, they tried to sleep but kept hearing the sounds of popping embers. In the morning, while their home was safe, houses all along Dume Drive were on fire. Still, there were no firefighters. Judy didn't see any until late in the day on Saturday, over twenty-four hours after the fire had crossed into Point Dume.

On Sunday morning, as Judy was walking her dog, she saw her friend, Dru Jacobsen, setting up tables in the parking lot at the Point Dume Elementary School. One table was covered with items like granola bars and dried foods. Another had sundries including bandages, diapers, and pet food. Judy had Brian bring over more tables. Soon everyone in Malibu began dropping off supplies at what became known as the Point Dume Relief Center. After the no-show of the fire department, the locals realized that the cavalry wasn't coming to rescue them—or to feed them. The fire department hadn't even allowed the Red Cross in, as the area wasn't deemed safe. Judy, Dru, and a handful of other women became the de facto disaster relief team for the neighborhood and eventually most of the city.

Open from 7:00 a.m. to 9:00 p.m., the Relief Center served coffee and three meals a day to an average of 150 people daily. People had to sign in and leave their addresses, which gave an indication of head count so the center could be prepared for future meals. The lists also enabled the center to check on individuals, especially the elderly, if they didn't return. Many of those who stayed behind were seniors with nowhere else to go.

The LA County Sheriff's Department had set up roadblocks to prevent anyone from getting in or out of the city, but there were also roadblocks *within* the city. Ostensibly, they were designed to keep looters out, but they also kept out residents who wanted to return to their neighborhood. The sheriffs didn't care if someone was a resident and had the ID to prove it. One elderly woman had heard a gas station was open in mid-Malibu. Anxious about being low on fuel, she went to fill up. On the way back she was stopped at a roadblock. She had to abandon her car and walk on foot past the checkpoint where she waited in the hopes that a neighbor could pick her up and drive her home. Fortunately, someone did.

The sheriffs didn't seem to grasp that those who stayed behind had saved hundreds of homes, possibly even preventing the fire from moving into the eastern part of the city. They often acted like the locals were getting in their way, not appearing to appreciate the fact that most Malibuites had seen no first responders during the fire. And now the first responders that residents *were* seeing were acting like the "gestapo," as one city council member called them.

Malibu City Manager Reva Feldman had lobbied for the National Guard to monitor the checkpoints rather than the sheriffs. She had seen the Guard in action during the 2017 Santa Rosa fires when she went there to assist. Impressed with how they handled the situation, she texted Governor Brown and then spoke with Governor-elect Newsom to get her request approved. But the LA County Sheriff, Jim McDonnell, didn't want the National Guard in his territory. He was locked in a tight battle for reelection against Alex Villaneuva. Though the election had been on November 6, the vote was still too close to call. Perhaps he thought he would look weak to his supporters if he allowed the Guard in.

"We don't need it," Feldman told me McDonnell said to her. "I'll send you an army."

It wasn't the one Feldman wanted.

Since getting into Malibu was nearly impossible, those who wanted back resorted to alternate modes of transportation. Namely, the Pacific Ocean, like Nate and Jackie had. On that Sunday, I was texting with Cris Garvin, a surfer and family friend, who lived on Point Dume but had evacuated to Santa Monica. He had a lead on a boat leaving out of Marina Del Rey, which was taking supplies into Malibu. Apparently, boats were unloading by the pier in Paradise Cove, an hour ride up the coast. The supplies were then taken to the Point Dume Relief Center, a ten-minute drive away. Cris didn't have a firm time or even a commitment that the boat would be there—or whether there would be room for him on it.

When Cris arrived at the boat's slip in the marina, there were a few others looking to hitch a ride. Cris helped load the boat with water, food, and gas, along with shovels, fire extinguishers, and medicines. An hour later at Paradise Cove, the Santa Ana winds were blowing hot and dry. The smoke was so bad everyone on the boat had to put on masks. The skipper asked if anyone could operate the eight-foot dinghy to shuttle the supplies onto the beach, and Cris volunteered.

As Cris set off for the beach, a sheriff on the bow of one of the department's boats eyed him warily. Cris had heard boaters were being threatened with arrest for bringing supplies ashore. He ignored the sheriff's glare and gunned the engine, driving the dinghy right onto the sand, where a group of young men swarmed him. The Point Dume Bombers weren't there to arrest him, however, but to unload the supplies. Cris made another seven or eight trips that day. The sheriffs never did a thing to stop him.

The first few days of the operation were smooth. But on Tuesday, larger numbers of boats started showing up with massive amounts of people who seemed to display a "look at me, I'm helping" attitude, and chaos erupted on the beach. Simeon Sturges, who'd saved the Paradise Cove mobile home park, described how one guy bringing in water threw bottles toward the beach, as if people might die of dehydration before he got to the sand. One of the bottles struck someone in the head.

The press had gotten word of the Relief Center's efforts. The fact that Sean Penn delivered ice every morning might have had something to do with it. Drones hovered in the air to make sure plenty of video existed for news reports and social media. Late night talk show hosts showed up to laud the "heroes" delivering supplies. Conan O' Brien cornered Simeon on the beach and shoved a microphone in his face.

"How many loads have you delivered today?" a grinning O'Brien asked, as if a prize might be presented to the person who'd lugged in the most food.

"I've been here for five days straight, asshole."

The mic was quickly pulled away.

Shortly after every news organization in the world showed up, someone else did too. The city manager, Reva Feldman. Someone many felt had been missing in action during the fire.

Since the entire city had been ordered to evacuate, Feldman and her staff did too, even though the City Hall building was in mid-Malibu and undamaged from the fire. City Hall even had power and Internet, unlike all of western Malibu. Judy Merrick wanted to know why Feldman wasn't in Malibu working at City Hall. Why wasn't the Red Cross being allowed in? Why wasn't Feldman organizing supplies for the Relief Center? Or at least, helping the center get people past roadblocks that were willing to bring in supplies? Or better yet, getting the sheriffs to let locals with proper identification in and out? Judy had constant problems getting food, water, and other critical supplies like medicine past the roadblocks, despite the fact that the center was also serving food to first responders. Although the sheriffs made only token efforts to block supplies from coming in on water, they were far stricter on land.

But the question Judy most would've liked to ask?

Why was Feldman showing up only now?

Judy had a sense it had to do with the press being there; Feldman likely didn't want to miss out on the chance to look good for the cameras, though no good look could exist for the collapse of an entire city government. Judy had expected failures during an event of the magnitude of the Woolsey Fire but not failures at *every* level: fire, police, all forms of government.

Feldman seemed even to resent the presence of the volunteers at the Relief Center, Judy told me. With no help from the real government, community members had come together to create their own. The fire and its fallout quickly acquired a nickname. Locals called it the YOYO Fire, for *You're On Your Own*.

One week in, the city finally did send something.

Two Porta Potties.

Point Dume Bombers and other locals unloading supplies from the many boats that came to help.

PHOTO JACK PLATNER

Horses and other large animals running free at Zuma Beach.
PHOTO DAVE TEEL

13

BEACH ON FIRE

John Zimpleman is a captain with the LA County Lifeguards, a division of the fire department. He's in his late thirties but he looks much younger with his thick black hair and chiseled features. Perhaps it has something to do with the fresh ocean air at Zuma Beach where John works. Like most lifeguards, he is into anything that involves the water: surfing, diving, fishing.

The Thursday the Woolsey Fire started was his sixth wedding anniversary. He'd planned a big, fancy dinner at his wife's favorite steakhouse. He even had a gift certificate. With the fires burning in the area, however, John thought it would be "a bad idea to leave home."

That Friday, he arrived early for his 7:00 a.m. shift at lifeguard headquarters, a run-down wood structure built in 1975 with a commanding view of the ocean. But on this day, John wasn't looking for swimmers in distress or people drinking beer on the beach. He turned in the opposite direction to search for flames. Already, he could see plumes of black smoke in the Santa Monica Mountains above Zuma Beach.

By 9:00 a.m., people started arriving at Zuma's parking lot. The mandatory evacuation had been ordered shortly before, but the twenty-mile span of the

PCH from Santa Monica to Point Dume quickly became gridlocked. Many asked John—and the Ocean Lifeguard Specialists who worked under him—whether the highway was safe.

"What if the flames burn over the PCH?" a mother with a nine-month-old infant asked. "What do I do? How do I escape?"

John's mentors had taught him the best thing to do in their line of work was to stay calm and say it was going to be okay. He took a deep breath and gave the woman a reassuring smile, offering her and the baby refuge inside the building, something he wasn't supposed to do. A number of elderly folks showed up at Zuma Beach with similar concerns, some dragging oxygen canisters. John took them in as well.

Though the sky over the ocean remained blue, massive clouds of black smoke dominated the horizon. At 11:00 a.m., cars started pouring into the lot. People brought their pets—not only dogs and cats but also sheep, pigs, and goats. Trailers arrived packed with horses from Malibu Park, the equestrian center of the city. Some people rode their horses to the beach; others had let their animals go free. Many of the released horses found their way to Zuma Beach.

Because the busy summer tourist season was over, most lifeguard towers sat empty, clumped together on the sand. Horses and other large animals like llamas and alpacas clustered around the towers, tied to various posts and protrusions. John and the other lifeguards worked with the owners to create a makeshift corral next to a giant sand dune.

Firehawk helicopters began to land on the helipad at Zuma to retrieve water from a fire engine stationed there, which was hooked up to a hydrant. At one point, a horse broke free and raced across the landing zone. People screamed at the impending catastrophe. At the last possible moment, the terrified animal was apprehended and moved to safety. When the fire engine got called away, John filled the helicopter tanks from the hydrant himself, something he'd never done before.

Later, using his binoculars, he spotted the fire that was tearing through Malibu Park. The fire had become so large that it created its own weather pattern. Black clouds began to circle, churning faster and faster, until the flames turned into a tornado. John watched in horror as the firenado ripped the roof off a house throwing it down the hillside like a Frisbee at the beach. The house then exploded as if a bomb was inside. Three people next door jumped off their deck to get away from the flames. John was sure they were going to die, but to his relief, they scrambled to safety.

More and more houses burned. The flames covered the hillsides for miles in either direction. John heard reports saying that the fire front was fourteen miles long. He wondered if the headquarters building—and the people protected inside—could burn.

What if we're not safe here?

In the doomsday event that the lifeguard station caught on fire, John was trained to move all vehicles and watercraft onto the sand, remove as much equipment as possible from inside the building, and turn off the utilities. The lifeguards would then rendezvous on the sand near Tower 2, which was the widest part of the beach and so furthest from the flames. But when John looked outside his glass windows, he estimated that there were over 5,000 people in his parking lot.

What do we do with them?

He and the other lifeguards crafted plans to evacuate the vehicles and, more importantly, the people—though most were sheltering inside their cars because the smoke was so thick. On top of moving people (and animals) as well as gauging the direction of the fire, John had the phone to worry about. The landline inside the headquarters building rang off the hook. Cellular communications had mostly failed as many cell towers were melted.

"Can you please check on my Dad? He's in the parking lot."

"I need to know if my mom made it out alive."

John and his team did the best they could, though in many cases, it was impossible to find people in the chaos of the parking lot. A call came in that people at a home on the beach a mile up the coast were running into the ocean to avoid the fire. John sent a Baywatch boat to rescue them and wondered if boats might have to evacuate the people in his parking lot.

Tony Johnston and Ryan Amechi, two of John's lifeguards, were sent to the western end of Zuma, where the smoke was thickest, to assist the LA County Fire Department with the staging and allocation of incoming firefighters and engines from outside areas.

"This is what we have," they'd radio the command center. "Where do you want them?"

Nearby, shrubs in the sand crackled with flames. Even the beach was on fire. When the smoke grew so thick the men couldn't see, they moved the staging effort across the PCH to the parking lot at the Trancas Shopping Center. Tony and Ryan did this job for thirty-six hours straight.

That evening, John could see home after home burning in the hills, lighting up the sky. On the radio, there were reports of widespread looting. The fire was bringing out the worst in people, so John made a decision to break protocol and do things he wasn't authorized to do.

He left his post to check on an elderly resident, Frank Brooks, a retired lifeguard. His son had called the headquarters concerned about his father's safety. Apparently, Frank had packed his wife's car with belongings and said he'd be following right behind her but never showed up to meet her.

The ride up into the Malibu Park neighborhood was "sketchy" with brush on both sides of the road engulfed in flames. A power pole was on fire. Power lines littered the streets. John tried three different routes before he made it to Calpine Drive. Most of the homes on the street were gone, but somehow Frank had saved his. He wore a scuba tank part of the time while fighting the fire and had never actually planned on leaving. Though the firestorm had blown through, he still wouldn't evacuate. John left him food and water since the pumps in the neighborhood no longer worked.

John stayed up all night answering the phone and doing welfare checks. When Saturday morning finally came, City Manager Reva Feldman and other city council members arrived and brought water and food for the hundreds who'd spent the night in their cars. She also arranged for transportation of the large animals. While some believed Feldman's help was motivated by her desire for good publicity, others who saw her in action, like John, disagreed.

The truth was more complicated.

Feldman was initially willing to help residents in any way she could. But a few days after the fire, she began to feel differently. She told me that residents who stayed behind should have evacuated Malibu, at the latest, by Monday or Tuesday when the fire was (sort of) under control. She believed those who stayed on after that needed to be prepared with food and water, and if they weren't, then that was on them, not her, nor the city of Malibu. She was forgetting, however, that people wanted to stay (or return) because fires could easily be stirred up, especially if the winds picked up again. It only takes one ember to burn down a house. When I returned eight days after the fire, properties were still smoldering. Feldman was also ignoring the reports of looting, another reason residents didn't want to leave.

Oblivious to the brewing controversy, John spent a good deal of the day delivering food and water, as well as $80,000 in generators, which had been purchased by a man whose name John didn't get. People, regular citizens, were doing things without expecting anything in return, least of all recognition for their efforts.

That Saturday night around ten o'clock, John and Ryan were driving around Point Dume looking for anyone who needed help. They came across a woman in her eighties who'd pulled over because the road ahead was blocked by downed power lines. Madeleine Radoff was exhausted and disoriented. She'd spent Friday night in her car in the Zuma Beach parking lot, but now she was trying to get home to see if her house survived. But the Point Dume neighborhood was still burning; it was too dangerous for her to be driving around. John and Ryan escorted her to Zuma Beach and had her park next to the headquarters building. They gave her food and water and let her use the restroom inside. John helped her settle in for another night in her car. He also got the phone number of her son.

"Knock on the door if you need anything," John said. "We'll be here all night."

The lifeguards certainly weren't getting any sleep. The landline continued to ring nonstop. He called the woman's son, who'd driven up from San Diego when he lost contact with his mother. But, like everyone else, he had been stopped at one of the checkpoints into Malibu. Until John's call, the son had no idea if his mother was alive.

On Sunday, John and Ryan offered to drive Madeleine to meet her son at the Las Posas checkpoint in Ventura County. Because the checkpoint was outside LA County, the lifeguards weren't allowed to take her there. They could be suspended or have reprimands placed in their files, which would prevent any future promotions or transfers. Lifeguards are trained to follow orders and never break rank. By escorting Madeleine to safety, the men were violating both. But they no longer cared about the rules. What was right was more important.

Ryan drove her car while she rode in John's lifeguard truck. Both men were concerned about her ability to drive. But Madeleine would only agree to leave if she could see her home first.

"I need to know if it's gone," she said.

John was apprehensive; he'd been with so many people Friday and Saturday who lost their homes. He was worried about the effect it might have on Madeleine's fragile state.

"I can't believe it," she said when they pulled up and saw that her house was still standing.

He wasn't sure who was more relieved—Madeleine or him.

Later, at the checkpoint, a man flagged them down. Madeleine got out and hugged her son. John choked up at the scene. The son gave both men hugs too. He wanted their names so he could call someone to have them recognized for their efforts, but John said it wasn't necessary. He also didn't want to advertise that they'd driven out of the county without authorization.

As they prepared to cross back through the checkpoint, dozens of people swarmed them, begging to go with them. Because people were desperate to check on family members and because the lifeguard division is part of the fire department, residents could get inside with John and Ryan. But there were so many people, way too many. How could they take one and not another? John drove away feeling helpless and miserable.

On the way back, the lifeguards stopped when they spotted smoke on the highway around Nicholas Canyon County Beach. The long timber staircase which went from the upper parking lot to the lower lot had been destroyed. A shimmering blue puddle was all that remained of the beach's Porta Potti. Smoldering groundcover on the hillside threatened to ignite the lifeguard tower that overlooked the ocean. Using shovels, they removed the ice plants and some shrubs nearby. As they were doing so, they suddenly realized they could see the nearby Chumash Village. The large trees and brush previously blocking it from view had burned to the ground.

A recreation of an authentic Native American village, the center sat on a four-acre site adjacent to Nicholas Canyon. The Chumash had lived in Malibu from 5,000 BC and so certainly knew about wildfires. Maybe that explained why their village didn't burn. Although they were constructed with highly flammable palm fronds, three Chumash dwellings, known as "ap aps," stood untouched by the firestorm.

On the way to their vehicle, John stopped dead.

"Look at that!" he said, pointing at something else.

Down on the sand was a perfectly straight line where the burning ice plant had been put out. The only thing that had stopped the Woolsey Fire was the high tide of the Pacific Ocean.

The only thing left standing at most homes was the chimney.
Somehow the tire swing made it too.
PHOTO ROBERT KERBECK

14

MARLBORO MAN

Best known as the Marlboro Man in print ads in the late '80s, Jefferson "Zuma Jay" Wagner was one of the five Malibu City Council members at the time of the Woolsey Fire. Jefferson, who's now in his mid-sixties, runs a successful surf shop on the PCH. I bought my son Davis's first wetsuit there when he was a toddler. A man of diverse talents to go with his 6'2" frame and rugged good looks, Jefferson wrote a book on the history of surfboard wax and stepped in to organize the revitalization of the iconic Malibu Pier when it fell into disrepair. Today, a trip to Malibu isn't complete without a visit to the Pier.

Jefferson has yet another skill set. He is a pyrotechnic expert.

His company, Movie Arms Management, is responsible for the special effects on feature films like *Volcano*, *Dante's Peak*, and *Pirates of the Caribbean*. He has a special effects license from Cal-Fire, the state firefighting organization. Jefferson has worked on over 200 films in a variety of capacities: weapons handler, special effects coordinator, pyrotechnician, and occasionally, stuntman.

So it was no surprise when, on November 9, as the Woolsey Fire approached Malibu, Jefferson didn't follow the mandatory evacuation order, which carries even more weight because of his role as a city council member. When they are elected, council members are given binders with instructions on what to do in an emergency. They basically come down to "get the hell out of the way" said Laura Rosenthal, another council member. Once an emergency is declared, city officials like Wagner and Rosenthal have no authority. The sheriff and fire departments are in command. They don't want elected officials getting in their way.

Instead, Jefferson prepared to put his movie set experiences to a real-life test. Shortly after 8:00 a.m., he began spreading out his 1,000 feet of fire hose, a process firefighters call "flaking." Jefferson flaked his hoses from side to side so, when charged with water, the line would make sweeping "S" curves, eliminating the possibility of kinks, while also making it easier to move the heavy lines since every second counted in a fire.

He hooked into the hydrant directly across the street using a splitter device to give him the potential to use two hoses. Most of his Latigo Canyon neighbors were driving over his hose lines as they fled from the fire so he placed two-by-fours alongside them to protect them. The weight of a car could burst a fully charged hose.

By 9:00 a.m., practically everyone was gone, including Guns 'N' Roses lead singer Axl Rose. The rocker had tall, highly flammable pine trees on his property, which sat in a fire-sensitive canyon in a wildfire-prone part of the state. Jefferson and others had requested that Rose remove them, but he'd refused. The proliferation of trees like his increased the amount of fuel available for fires, increasing the danger to everyone in the area.

In his backyard, Jefferson set up a fire pump for his 50,000-gallon pool and used another splitter to give him two more hoses. This way he wouldn't be dependent on the water department's hydrants.

At 9:30 a.m., he went inside and threw on his fire-fighting brushland suit, respirator mask, and goggles with heat-release flap. He and his long-time girlfriend, Candace Brown, had just paid off the mortgage on their home. They weren't going down without a fight.

At sixty-eight years old and 110 pounds, Candace wasn't strong enough to handle the hoses, but that didn't mean she wasn't going to pull her weight.

While Jefferson would stay outside to fight the fire, she would fight any flames inside or near the house using movie set fire extinguishers. Jefferson kept twelve extra-large CO2 extinguishers in various locations in their home. He had one in practically every room.

"I live in a fire zone," he told me. "You don't want water in your house unless you have to." He explained that CO2 didn't damage furniture or clothes or even people. The highly pressurized (and cold) CO2 simply took away the oxygen necessary for a fire to burn.

Candace spotted the first flames at 10:25 a.m., though it was hard to see them through the cloud of gray smoke billowing toward the heavens. What sounded like loud raindrops were really pops from trees and plants being ravaged by the spreading inferno. Soon 200-foot flames covered the hillsides, dwarfing the telephone poles, threatening not only their home but their lives. Jefferson wielded the hoses, ducking flames that shot over his head while lobbing water onto his house from all directions. Occasionally, he turned the hose on himself because of the "pure, intense heat." Candace ran around outside lugging the heavy CO2 cylinders up and down stairs to blast fires on their decks.

When the initial firestorm passed through, they were euphoric. Candace shouted down from their deck, "We made it! We made it!"

"Fucking yes," Jefferson yelled up, the wildfire equivalent of the balcony scene from *Romeo and Juliet*. They whooped and hollered at each other.

Then they glanced toward Latigo Canyon Road and the ocean in the distance. There the skies had turned from gray to black, which meant it wasn't brush that was now burning but objects made by man. A sea of red dots was visible in the smoke, each one a fully engulfed home. They looked like jack o'lanterns in the dark, their doors and windows illuminated by the flames.

Axl Rose's place was still standing, though his pine trees had been incinerated, likely sending embers onto his neighbors' homes. That's the thing about flammable (and invasive) trees like pine, eucalyptus, and palm. Often the embers travel hundreds of yards, even miles. I witnessed the eucalyptus trees on my neighbor's property catch fire. A chunk broke off and hurtled across the sky like a meteor, landing a few houses away. Moments later, a fire sprouted from the landing spot. Shortly thereafter, flames engulfed that home.

Jefferson was jubilant they'd beaten the storm, but he knew it would only take one ember to burn down his house, so he remained vigilant. But his fire pump had become clogged by the debris that had fallen into his pool, much of it the remains of a neighbor's house. He had backups for most of his equipment, but he didn't have another $20 filter for the pump. As a result, he now had to rely on the water from the hydrant, which could go dry at any moment. Since the electricity was out in Malibu, the pumps to refill the tanks weren't working. Also, many evacuating homeowners had turned on their sprinklers before they left, as if having a wet lawn would save their home from burning down. Instead, it drained the tanks and handicapped those who stayed behind to fight the fire.

That afternoon, the hydrant water ran out.

Jefferson and Candace watched as gas lines from destroyed homes caught fire, exacerbating the danger. Walking the perimeter of his home, Jefferson discovered that while his home survived the initial onslaught, his fiberglass ladder hadn't. Parts of it were as thin as strands of spaghetti. Without the ladder, he wouldn't be able to get up on his roof. Sure enough, thirty minutes later, black smoke began to rise from the roof. In all his preparations and plans, he'd never considered needing a second ladder.

Candace wasn't strong enough to boost him up, and her small frame made standing on her shoulders an impossibility. He ran inside to the third floor where the ceiling paint was shimmering and blistering from the heat. He carried every remaining CO2 cylinder up the stairs and blasted the ceiling. The containers were meant to put out small fires on movie sets, not to save a house from a wildfire, but they were all he had.

Candace began to pack photos and personal items into her Fiat.

As she did, she spotted fire engines parked 250 yards down the street. She also realized she was injured. Carrying the CO2 containers had given her a hernia. A cut on her foot was inflamed, likely from running through toxic soot and ash to put out fires. She'd been wearing flip-flops because they were the fastest shoes to throw on (something my wife had done too) but now understood why firefighters wore boots.

Ignoring the pain, she hopped into the Fiat and approached one of the engines. The captain put down his window. His men were inside with him and the air conditioning was running. She explained that she and her boyfriend needed help fighting the fire.

"We can't go any further up into that canyon," the captain said. He was from outside the area, as were many firefighters fighting the fire.

"There's plenty of room to turn around," she said. "My boyfriend is on the Malibu City Council." She thought that information might get the firefighters to assist them.

"We're not assigned to that area."

"Please," she begged. "He needs to get on the roof. Our ladder burned."

"We don't have orders. Sorry."

"Are you kidding me? You guys are supposed to be firefighters."

"Sorry ma'am."

Candace went to each of the five or six engines pleading for help. In vain. Not a single captain would even get out of his engine.

"They're not coming," she said when she returned home. It was the hardest thing she'd ever had to accept since it meant all hope was gone. They'd saved every penny to build their dream home and it was going to burn down.

Jefferson realized it was time for Candace to evacuate, while she still safely could. Just before dark, exhausted and injured, Candace packed a few more pictures, grabbed the dog, and left. But Jefferson wasn't going to lose his home to a few embers, even though they were now burning holes in his ceiling.

He noticed that the hydrant hose outside would occasionally come to life, shooting water here and there, so Jefferson dragged the hose inside the house. Every once in a while, a short blast of water would come out and Jefferson would fire it at the ceiling. When the hydrant stopped working again, he'd shoot CO2 at the flames. He moved their furniture away from the flames to keep the inside of the house from catching fire. Hot tar from the melting roof dripped onto his back.

He had his fireman's coat on but that didn't protect him when the roof collapsed. Cinder blocks crashed down onto him, knocking him unconscious. The men who installed his satellite TV had used the blocks to hold down their equipment so it wouldn't blow away during strong winds. They hadn't considered what might happen during a fire.

When he came to, Jefferson could feel that the blocks, now covered in hot tar, had penetrated his clothing and burned his skin. He'd done everything he could to save his home. With an extra filter or ladder—or a firefighter's help—he might've done just that.

He stumbled into his Honda Pilot and drove over bricks from a chimney that had somehow ended up in the middle of the road. Dodging flames everywhere, he descended the 1,000-foot elevation from the canyon to the PCH. Along the way, he began to worry about the amount of smoke in the air. He was afraid the car filter would get clogged the way his pool filter had and cause the car to stall. He put the Honda in neutral to take in less smoke but kept the engine running, giving him power steering and control of the vehicle.

When he arrived at his surf shop, where Candace was waiting, he was "physically hacked." He couldn't take a breath without coughing. Candace thought he was going to die on the spot.

"You have to go to the hospital," she said when she saw his singed face.

But Candace couldn't see well enough to drive at night. Without electricity, they couldn't call 911, and all the cell towers had melted. Suddenly, Candace heard a beep from an electronic device and realized the power had come on. She grabbed the phone and dialed 911. Thirty seconds later, just after she'd relayed their position and Jefferson's injuries to the 911 operator, the power went out again.

It would not come back on for days.

The paramedics didn't even bother to assess Jefferson on site. They threw him into their ambulance and, sirens wailing, tore down the PCH toward UCLA Medical Center in Santa Monica. At the check-in, the nurse described his soot-filled hair as black when really it was gray. Jefferson spent three days in intensive care with carbon monoxide poisoning, eye contamination, and kidney issues from the toxins in his bloodstream.

Sheriffs found his firefighting jacket near the rubble of his home. Apparently, he'd thrown it off before he got into his car. Remnants of tar dotted the back, along with dozens of burn holes. The coat looked like a piece of Swiss cheese.

For weeks Jefferson struggled to recover from his injuries. Even when I interviewed him in his surf shop three months after the fire, he didn't seem himself. He walked slowly and had a slight limp. Candace needed to have a toe amputated from the infection she'd gotten while fighting the fire. Her doctor said she might have died had they not caught it in time. Jefferson and Candace had nearly died trying to save their home, when all they needed was a boost onto the roof.

"If someone had been willing to do this," Jefferson said, linking his fingers and cupping his hands together in the classic leg-up gesture, "I would've saved our house."

He shrugged his head and went back to ordering surfboards but, before he did, he wanted to show me something else. He pulled out a binder full of colored charts and diagrams.

"It's the evacuation plan I'm working on," he said. "Next time there will be eight zones in Malibu. Each will have its own evacuation location. This way the highway won't become gridlocked."

Jefferson had added a new skill to his already impressive set: traffic planner.

Gaping holes in the collapsing Triunfo Creek Bridge

PHOTO MORGAN RUNYON

15

THE OLD PLACE

In the town of Cornell in the Agoura Hills area near Malibu, the Old Place looks like a saloon out of the Wild West. A classic roadhouse made entirely of wood, the structure has a front porch, a long antique bar with benches for seating, five booths, and a handful of tables. Over the front door is a massive set of deer antlers.

The owner, Morgan Runyon, never thought he'd be fighting a fire to save the Old Place. At various times during his life, he'd kind of hoped the thing *would* burn down. He certainly had no desire to run the family restaurant. He had a wife and two small children and a successful career as an art director for TV shows and commercials.

Morgan's father, Tom, had purchased the building in 1970 and converted it from a country store to a restaurant. The structure dated to 1884 and had once served as the town of Cornell's post office. For close to forty years, there were only two items on the menu: steak and clams.

The limited options didn't stop folks from coming; even famous movie stars like Steve McQueen (who tended bar and occasionally washed the dishes), Jason Robards, Katherine Ross, Ali McGraw, and Burgess Meredith found their way to the ramshackle spot. For them and other celebrities, the Old Place was a "getaway," which also happens to be the title of a Steve McQueen film that Tom Runyon had a part in. His Hollywood friends liked Tom so much, they insisted he be cast in their films.

The Hell's Angels could regularly be seen chowing down on the huge steaks Tom and his wife, Barbara, cooked over oak. Though the gang members were welcome, their colors were not. Tom required they leave their Hell's Angels vests outside with their bikes. Other frequent guests included the heavy equipment operators constructing the 101 Freeway and, of course, the local residents, the majority of whom were actual cowboys.

While his parents cooked dinners and tended bar, Morgan recalled sleeping in a van with his sister outside the restaurant when they were little. He also remembered his father's mantra on wildfires: *There will be a fire, it will burn to the ocean, and no one will be there to help you.*

As his parents aged, the restaurant became quirkier and quirkier. Sometimes Tom and Barbara forgot to buy food. The hours of operation became sporadic. By 2009, the Old Place was barely open and the real estate vultures started circling. One wanted to turn the restaurant into a "cowboy sushi bar."

In a world where so much had changed in forty years, the Old Place remained exactly the same. For Morgan, it was a vestige of California's frontier past and a living piece of history. When Tom died in July, 2009 at the age of eighty-nine, Morgan found himself wanting to preserve it.

"Are you crazy?" his wife Fran said when he told her. "You've got a great job. You get to surf whenever you want."

His sister was blunter. "Are you dumb?"

And his mother reminded him, "You have a young family. Did you forget how hard that was on everyone?"

Morgan felt he would be failing his father's legacy if he didn't try. At first, he didn't think it was his thing, but within a year, he came to realize that continuing the family tradition was an amazing gift. He wasn't going to get rich but he could make a living.

And he could make the Old Place better.

He expanded the menu and built a wine store/tasting room next door. Magazines and newspapers raved about the "fascinating steakhouse that time forgot." The *LA Times* described the Old Place as "warm and welcoming—and fun." The critic added, "everyone I've brought has declared it one of their favorite restaurants ever."

As business boomed, Morgan didn't fool himself it was the food or the drinks or the service that had crowds lined up outside the door. It was the old-timey setting, one he could never replicate should the building burn down. Current building codes wouldn't allow for the "tinderbox" to be rebuilt. And that is why on Thursday afternoon, when he heard about the two fires headed his way, Morgan drove to the top of one of the tunnels on Kanan Dume Road. From there, he could tell the Hill Fire was burning toward Point Mugu and wasn't a threat. But the huge plume of smoke coming his way from the Woolsey Fire made him nervous.

He left the Old Place early that night for his home in Topanga Canyon.

"The wind direction doesn't look good for the restaurant," he told Fran.

On Friday, he got up at 4:00 a.m. and put on jeans, wool socks, a thick jacket, and good boots. He'd fought five fires in his lifetime and knew the importance of being prepared. He loaded his Dodge Ram truck with shovels, fire extinguishers, chain saws, 1,000 feet of fire hose, and two fire pumps. Driving toward the restaurant, he saw an orange glow, as if the sun was rising in the wrong spot, and knew he was in for trouble. When he arrived, his line chef, Greg, was prepping the day's meals.

"Why don't you wrap it up?" Morgan said.

"What? No, I can't. I gotta get all the food ready for the weekend."

"There's not going to be a weekend."

Twenty minutes later the power went off.

"I'll take the food home and finish prepping it there," said Greg.

"Sounds good." Morgan knew the fire was coming and that most of the food would be wasted or given away. He stretched his hoses across the street to the hydrant on the other side but didn't hook into it. Maybe a fire engine would show up, he thought, then reminded himself of his father's philosophy. People were driving by the restaurant, honking and shouting, "Get out! It's coming!"

Many stopped to ask him, "What are you doing?"

"I'm staying," he said.

"Why?"

Morgan wanted to explain that certain things could be repaired or rebuilt with insurance money but a building from 1884 wasn't one of them. Instead, he said, "I have a plan."

Though he didn't.

Shortly thereafter, Brian Tieleman pulled up. His girlfriend, Hollie, was an employee at the restaurant. She had already evacuated from their Malibou Lake home, and Brian had promised her he would do the same, but when he drove by the Old Place, he couldn't leave Morgan behind.

"Would you like some help?" Brian asked.

"God, yes."

The men prepped the property by placing barrels of water onto the wooden decks and moving anything that might burn away from the structures. Around 8:00 a.m., they heard the crackling of the approaching firestorm and took shelter inside the restaurant. Because Morgan was experienced with fighting fires, he knew this was the time to remain calm and stay safe. His father would've poured a drink but Morgan and Brian drank water.

Morgan knew the first moments after the storm passed were going to be critical. When the shaking of the building stopped, the men sprinted outside. The fire had spread across the entire property. Morgan and Brian rushed to put out embers and spot fires before they grew out of control. One mistake could make the difference between saving the restaurant—or losing it. The men had good water pressure and blasted the areas closest to the restaurant, then worked their way to the edges of the property. Had Morgan been alone, he wouldn't have been able to cover enough ground. The Old Place would have burned.

Miraculously, nothing of significance was destroyed.

But Morgan realized the fire was heading toward the home he'd grown up in on El Matador Beach. His ninety-year-old mother, Barbara, still lived there alone. He reprimanded himself for not thinking to evacuate her the night before. Morgan's grandmother, Cornelia, had purchased the property back in 1937 when May Rindge's company, Marblehead, started selling off pieces of her pristine Rancho Malibu.

"I gotta get to my mom," Morgan said.

"I should probably go check on my house too," Brian said.

"It's probably not there. You need to be prepared for that."

"I know."

"I'm so grateful you stopped."

The men hugged and went their separate ways. Morgan spotted a fire department pickup truck in front of the restaurant and asked for help.

"I gotta get my mom out. She lives at El Matador Beach."

Morgan hoped the fireman would call and get help or maybe the two of them would hop in his vehicle and drive to Malibu to get Barbara.

Instead, the guy, a fire department building inspector, not a frontline firefighter, said, "You don't need to worry. The fire's not going to make it there."

Dumb fuck, Morgan thought as his father's words echoed in his mind: the fire doesn't stop until it hits the ocean.

He turned away to head toward his truck.

A neighbor of the restaurant, Gary Jones, drove up and stopped.

"I lost everything," he said, clearly distraught. He'd lived in the area for over thirty years, almost as long as the Old Place was open. "House, garage, barns, all the birds, three of my dogs." He'd owned a number of birds including turkeys, chickens, peacocks, parrots, parakeets, and cockatiels.

"I'm so sorry," said Morgan.

"My Model T burned too."

Gary was often seen driving around the town in his 1918 Ford Model T

"Fuck it," he said and started to drive toward the Triunfo Creek Bridge.

"Wait," Morgan yelled, pointing at the creosote guardrails, which were ablaze. "The bridge is sagging. Look, there's smoke coming out of the asphalt."

"I don't care. I'm going." Gary hit the gas and the car zoomed toward the bridge. Morgan didn't want to watch his friend die. He turned away as the vehicle disappeared into a plume of black smoke. When he turned back, Gary had made it to the other side. Not long after, the bridge collapsed and would burn for days.

Gary might have been the last person to drive over it.

Morgan loaded the fire hose, a chainsaw, and a pump into his truck and made his way toward Kanan Dume Road to head toward his mother's house, but because the bridge was melting, he had to take the long way around. He passed the historic Paramount Ranch where scores of movies and TV shows had been filmed, including the HBO hit series, *Westworld.* Fire was tearing through the ranch completely razing the Old West sets.

At around 9:30 a.m., Morgan made it to the first tunnel on Kanan, but it was blocked by power lines from a sagging power pole, which was on fire. He turned back in dread, thinking his mother could die.

He drove toward the Old Place and watched the fire in his rearview mirror—until he realized the fire was coming from his truck. Embers had landed in the cab, igniting a bedroll he used as a sleeping bag. He pulled over and set it by the side of the road, making sure to position it so the bedroll wouldn't start any more fires.

Returning to the Old Place, he did a quick patrol of the property, spraying out the embers he found. At one point, he came upon two coveys of quail. Normally, the skittish birds take off at the sight of a human. But these birds parted as he walked through them, then regrouped and followed him, as if to say, *we're in this together.*

Morgan knew he couldn't stay. He had to reach his mom. But now his truck was causing him problems. A flashing red light was warning of an issue with the fuel rail pressure. He didn't know what the hell a fuel rail was but the truck kept shutting off. Each time it did, he had to coast over to the side of the road to stop and restart the vehicle.

He didn't think he could make it to his mother's, so he drove to the top of the tunnel at Kanan where he had cell service. Maybe he could get someone else to save her. He reached Fran who told him that his mother was safe, that neighbors had gotten her out. But Morgan still wanted to try to save the home that had been in his family since before World War II.

I'm too late, he kept thinking as he coasted down Kanan. At the bottom of the hill, a man was walking five mini-ponies along the Pacific Coast Highway. In the midst of flames, black smoke, and burning homes, the saving of the animals was "a beautiful sight."

His truck made it to the El Matador community. Immediately, he patrolled the neighborhood of fifteen to twenty homes. While his family home seemed safe, the property of musician Herb Alpert was on fire. Morgan unloaded the firehose and pump he'd brought and began fighting the flames. Others had stayed and together they worked to save the neighborhood using chainsaws to cut down trees that were about to burn. Just one tree on fire could cause the entire neighborhood to burn down.

When evening came, not one home had been lost, though Alpert's property suffered significant damage. Morgan began cramping from physical exhaustion and extreme dehydration. He went inside his mother's house and had a beer and some Halloween candy.

"The best meal I ever had," he said.

In the morning, he drove back to the Old Place, convinced it had burned up. Many homes that didn't burn in the initial firestorm were caught later by stray embers. To his joy, the building stood untouched by flames. The bridge Gary had driven over was buckled and had gaping holes in it. Natural gas spewed out of a broken line. An employee from the local water department stopped when he noticed Morgan had left his fire hose connected to the hydrant.

"Uh, sir, you can't hook into the hydrants. That's against the law."

Fuck you, Morgan thought. "Well, I wouldn't have," he said, his volume increasing with each word, "If somebody had been here to fight the fire. A firefighter, perhaps?" Some of the old-time cowboys in the town might have strung the worker up. To make sure the water department got his message, Morgan left the hose on the hydrant for days, long after the danger had passed.

While Morgan was glad he had stayed and saved the Old Place, his efforts came with a price. For weeks afterwards, he would wake up at 3:20 in the morning, as if he'd set an alarm. He was still on fire alert and unable to get back to sleep. Many who went through the Woolsey Fire described suffering from PTSD-like symptoms.

His ninety-year-old mother, however, wasn't fazed by the experience—or the loss of power for close to a month. After the '78 Kanan Fire, armed with a freezer full of venison, she cooked the meat in the ground.

Millie Decker and the homesteaders of Malibu would've been proud.

Melted electric meter

PHOTO GARDIA FOX

The singed opening page of I am Eloise.

PHOTO DAVE TEEL

16

I AM ELOISE

Nicole Fisher is a teacher at Juan Cabrillo Elementary School. She teaches art classes to children from kindergarten through fifth grade, including my son, Davis, when he attended school there. I met Nicole's husband, Dave Teel, when he worked as a teller at the local bank. Dave had been a professional fashion photographer for years; he took my headshots for my author's website.

Nicole and Dave moved to the Malibu Highlands area off Latigo Canyon Road in 2007. Theirs was a merged family home. They'd met in 2001 when they both lived in the Beverlywood area of Los Angeles. Dave's wife at the time, Marcy, was suffering from Non-Hodgkin Lymphoma. While she was in the hospital for a second stem cell transplant, Marcy read an article in the *LA Times* called "Saving the School Down the Street," which detailed Nicole's efforts to restore Canfield Elementary, a school Nicole had attended as a child. A group of parents had come together to raise money to buy a new library and a playground. A theatre program was started.

"I want our kids to go to that school," Marcy told Dave.

They lived ten blocks outside the district, so they enrolled using the address of Marcy's sister since she lived inside the school's boundaries. In August 2001, at the kindergarten welcome picnic, Nicole was writing name tags for the kids, including her own kindergartener, Hayley, when Dave walked up.

"My daughter's name is Alex," he said.

Nicole wrote out a name tag with the traditional spelling.

"No, it's Allyx," he said, correcting her spelling.

It was the only conversation they had.

Nicole had a longer conversation with Marcy, who was quite ill. She had no hair. Her left arm was paralyzed.

"I'm going to be fine," she said. "I'm going to beat this."

One month later, Marcy, Dave, Allyx, and their two-year-old son, Adam, flew to Michigan for a surprise sixtieth birthday party for her mom, a party Marcy had planned from her hospital bed. At 4:00 a.m. the night after the party, Marcy began to have breathing issues. Dave rushed the family home to Los Angeles on September 10, 2001 and took Marcy straight to Cedars-Sinai Hospital.

Three days later she slipped into a coma.

"You're not going to get out of the hospital this time," said one not-so-kind doctor, who turned out to be right. On October 1, Dave made the gut-wrenching decision to remove life support and let Marcy go.

After the funeral in Michigan, Dave and his children flew back to Los Angeles. He was unsure whether to stay in California or return home to Michigan. In their house, he felt Marcy's presence telling him to stay. Canfield Elementary rallied behind Dave and his kids. Women brought over food, including containers of homemade lasagna too big to fit in his refrigerator. Allyx had missed the first month of school, but Nicole and others got her caught up and enrolled her in Girl Scouts. The first real interaction Dave and Nicole had was outside the principal's office on the day of a school walking tour of the local bank. Dave didn't know the kids needed to be wearing a Canfield Elementary shirt and Allyx didn't have one.

I gotta find this kid a shirt, Nicole thought.

She searched the entire school until she found a spare shirt for Allyx. Over the course of the school year, Allyx and Nicole's daughter, Hayley, became friends. They had playdates together. The next year in first grade, they were classmates.

Nicole had been separated from her husband and she and Dave began to date in secret. They weren't sure what their families would think. After a year, they told their kids. Allyx and Hayley thought it was cool and fantasized about the possibility of becoming sisters. They already shared the same middle name, though Allyx's was Rachael and Hayley's was Rachel. Why not share parents too? But Nicole's middle child, Lucas, wasn't happy about the turn of events.

"What about my Dad?" he asked.

Dave's son, Adam, was upset as well. Though he had no memory of his mother that didn't mean he wanted her replaced. A lot of therapy—and headbutting—ensued.

Nicole wasn't sure she wanted to get married again but felt Dave's kids needed a mom. She knew what it was like to grow up without a parent. While her father wasn't dead, he had run off with his secretary when Nicole was nine.

In 2006, Dave and Nicole married, and the Teel family moved into her tiny Beverlywood home. Allyx, Hayley, and Nicole's youngest daughter, Katie, shared one room, while the boys shared another. Nicole spotted an ad for a good-sized home in Malibu far enough from the beach and high enough up in the canyon to make it affordable. The property had a small pool with a water slide and a treehouse. Each kid could have their own room. The elementary, middle, and high school in Malibu are all on the same campus, so the kids would be close to each other no matter what grade they were in. It seemed the perfect place to give their blended family a fresh start and its own identity.

A year after they purchased the property, the crash of 2008 came. The stock market tumbled thousands of points in days. Businesses stopped spending and began to look for ways to cut costs. One of those costs was advertising. Dave's fashion clients began cancelling shoots. His business disappeared practically overnight.

The loss of a five-day shoot for Ugg Outerwear was particularly devastating. He needed that money to pay his mortgage. He went for a bike ride to blow off steam, but when he returned from the ride, he was having chest pain. He had to sit on the porch for a long while because he didn't have the energy to walk into the house.

Finally, he gathered the strength to stand and walked slowly to a table with his computer. Nicole was on the opposite side working on her computer.

"You don't look good," she said, peering around her screen to stare at him.

"I don't feel good." Dave was afraid to admit what he feared might be happening. He kept hoping the chest pain would go away, but it was getting worse.

Something about her husband's face and body language was off—very off. "I'm taking you to urgent care. Right now," Nicole said.

It took the doctor thirty seconds to determine Dave was having a heart attack. He was rushed by ambulance to Saint John's hospital in Santa Monica where emergency surgery was performed and a stent put in. In the course of the operation, one of his arteries was accidently torn, resulting in severe complications. Nicole feared Allyx and Adam were going to lose their remaining biological parent. Another stent had to be put in. During the recovery, his heart had to be flushed every four hours, causing him to scream in pain each time. Nicole told him to write letters to his kids "just in case."

Dave survived his scare and took a job at the local bank. Despite the hurdles (and expenses) of his near-death experience and the collapse of the global economy, Dave and Nicole were able to hang onto their home. As the Great Recession became a distant memory, Dave even got some photography gigs again. By November 2018, their youngest daughter, Katie, a senior, was the only child living in the house. Their goal was to pay for the home until she graduated in June. Perhaps then they would sell the home (and reduce the financial pressure) and move to Michigan.

But then came the Woolsey Fire. On Thursday, Nicole heard about the fires on the other side of the hill. She wanted her family to pack and evacuate that evening. Katie had a test in the morning and found her mother's concerns annoying. Dave, too, thought Nicole was overreacting—until he remembered his wife had known he was having a heart attack before he did. They filled three cars with stuff and went to spend the night at a friend's home in Malibu West.

Nicole didn't sleep, though, and watched the fire on the news all night. At 7:30 a.m., she and Dave drove back to load another car full of stuff. The wind was perfectly still, but an orange glow filled the sky behind their house.

"Dave," she said, "We're going to lose our home."

What can I not replace? she wondered. Then, *what can I carry?*

Nicole first grabbed the baby books of each child, forgetting to get her own baby book. She rescued all of the children's yearbooks, except for Lucas's. It was a no-win scenario. Trying to decide—or remember—what to take was "surreal." She tried to be present with her split-second decisions but in retrospect "wished she could do it over again." She forgot Lucas's saxophone and two guitars. She left behind Katie's vinyl record collection. Hayley had a pair of Frye boots that Nicole didn't remember. The boots were well over the family's budget, so Hayley received the money for one boot on her birthday and the money for the other on Christmas.

But certain things she did not forget, despite the growing glow from the fire.

Marcy had given Alex a pillow when he was a baby, which he called his "mommy pillow." Nicole made sure to grab it. Allyx had a stuffed animal called "Bunny," given to her when Marcy died. Nicole saved that too, along with Marcy's jewelry box.

She searched for the books she'd read to the kids when they were little, but she couldn't find the girls' favorite, *Eloise*. The story of a precocious six-year-old who lives on the "tippy-top" floor of the Plaza Hotel in New York, the book was Nicole's favorite as well. She admired Eloise's sense of adventure but felt empathy too, given Eloise seemed abandoned by her parents and was incredibly lonely, just as Nicole had felt as a girl.

But she couldn't find the book and the fire was now just over the ridge. Nicole and Dave sped away but not before stopping at the home of their friends, John and Jennifer Gonzalez, whose daughter, Nina, was best friends with Katie.

"It doesn't look good," Nicole said, gesturing to what looked like a second sunrise behind the Gonzalez's log cabin, a home they had built themselves. She knew John had a fire pump and was thinking of staying, but this appeared to be no ordinary fire.

"It's not too windy," John said. "I'm going to stay."

"I'm really concerned for you." Nicole was hoping she could talk him out of it.

Instead, John said, "You should stay."

Nicole had many skills, including blending families, but fighting fires wasn't one of them. She didn't want to risk getting trapped. She'd heard the stories on the news about people being burned alive in their cars at Paradise. If she was going to die, she wanted to do so at the beach.

Nicole and Dave never saw their home again, which burned along with the Gonzalez's log cabin. John gave saving it his best shot but his pump failed, and he was defenseless against the massive flames. The families ended up evacuated together at a hotel in Oxnard, along with another Malibu teacher who'd lost her home, Nancy Levy. The three families would gather together in Nicole and Dave's two-bedroom unit. Hayley, Allyx, and Katie joked that they felt like Eloise, though the Oxnard "suite" was a far cry from Eloise's penthouse at the Plaza. For them, the stay was an adventure, even if it came as the result of a tragedy. Nicole was grateful to have a glass of wine with good friends and colleagues to commiserate about what they'd lost.

When Nicole and Dave returned home, they searched for anything that might have survived. The Red Cross left sifters at burned-out homes. Made of wood with a mesh screen, residents used the sifters like old fashioned gold diggers to sort through the rubble. The fires burned so hot, over 2,000 degrees, that rarely did anything make it through. Most people sifted for a few hours and gave up. It was exhausting work, physically and emotionally, going through the charred remains of your home hoping to find that one thing that hadn't been destroyed.

Nicole found that one thing.

Wedged in the branch of a tree, she spotted a piece of partially burned paper. She figured it was junk or perhaps had blown into the tree from someone else's burned-down home. As she approached, she saw it was a drawing. She realized it was a page from the *Eloise* book. And not just any page, it was the opening page, which read:

I am Eloise. I am six.

The page gave Nicole a sense of hope in the midst of so much loss. But when the schools reopened six week later, she learned a colleague's husband had died, unrelated to the fire.

For the first time, Nicole broke down in tears.

Many of her students didn't return. Whether their homes had burned or the parents were concerned about air quality or the very real potential of mudslides, Nicole wasn't sure. But teaching—and the schools—weren't the same. Her students' artwork reflected this. One fourth grader painted what looked like the flaming eye of Sauron from *Lord of the Rings*. The girl was painting the fires she'd seen.

For Christmas, Nicole received the *Eloise* page in a glass frame. A reminder from her children that not everything had been lost.

Another Malibu home where nothing remained.

PHOTO ROBERT KERBECK

17

JOHNNY DRAMA

Kevin Dillon is best known for playing the character Johnny Drama in the hit HBO series *Entourage*, but he also starred in seminal films like *Platoon* and *The Doors*. He lives in a relatively modest, Spanish-style home in the Bonsall section of Malibu across from Zuma Beach. I met him when a mutual friend, Tommy Hill, invited me over to Kevin's to play ping-pong. And that's how the Malibu Table Tennis Club was born.

Starting in 2015, guys would show up, usually on Sundays, to battle it out on a table in Kevin's driveway surrounded by his collection of classic cars, including his favorite, "Bernadette," a 1969, baby-blue Camaro convertible. The core group consisted of Tommy; Chris Wynne, Kevin's property manager and friend; Damon Skelton, a local realtor; and me. Those nights reminded me of episodes from the *Entourage* series and often turned into large, boisterous parties. Judd Nelson, Patrick Warburton, and others played while Miss Hawaiian Tropic circa 2005 jumped on Kevin's trampoline in a bikini. Beer flowed but only light beer since Kevin and the other actors needed their abs to be screen ready at all times. I wasn't sure where I fit in the entourage and hoped I wasn't Turtle, the gofer character in the show.

When Tommy moved away in 2017, the Malibu Table Tennis Club fell apart. Still, I look back fondly on those times, particularly since I left as the reigning champ.

I was surprised to learn that Kevin had stayed behind to fight the Woolsey Fire. When I found out he'd done it alone, I was stunned. Kevin made his living on his looks. He was the last guy who could afford to get burned in a wildfire.

On the day of our interview, Kevin was hosting a birthday party for his long-time, live-in girlfriend, Shannon. She popped into the conversation once in a while to correct him whenever his information was off but just as often he corrected her. Sometimes he said something happened in the morning but Shannon said it happened in the afternoon or vice versa. The phenomenon wasn't unique to them. Nearly everyone I interviewed talked about the blur of time during the fire.

Kevin and Shannon were in bed at 1:00 a.m. on the night of the fire when he got a call from his ex-wife, Jane.

"You have to help me," she said. "The fire's coming here."

Jane lived in nearby Malibou Lake with their daughter, Ava. Kevin hopped into one of his less-collectible cars, a 2011 Camaro with little gas. On the way up Kanan Dume Road, he could already see flames. When he arrived at the house, Jane was still packing.

"There's no time. We gotta go," he said.

But Jane and Ava weren't leaving without their pets, which included three dogs, two cats, three rabbits, and a tarantula. Kevin wrangled the animals into his vehicle and grabbed his daughter. Jane followed them in her car.

On the way out of Malibou Lake toward the beach, flames consumed everything in their path—trees, homes, power poles. Ava stared out the window in what Kevin described as shock, watching the fire head in the same direction they were.

The group arrived at Kevin's home around two o'clock in the morning. Shannon steered Jane, Ava, and the animals to their guest room, but warned

Jane not to unpack. Having grown up in Malibu, Shannon had experienced fires before and knew to be ready to leave at a moment's notice.

Instead, Jane unpacked her car.

Kevin felt confident the fire wouldn't reach them, that the fire department would get control of the situation. But if they didn't, he wanted to be alert, so he lay down to get some sleep. Shannon woke him as the sun rose. Thick clouds of smoke, visible in the morning light, mushroomed above their house.

The group evacuated again, this time to Paradise Cove, a five-minute drive down the PCH. On the way, Kevin tried to get gas for the Camaro but was informed that all stations in Malibu were already out.

Later at Paradise Cove, he got a call from his manager.

"Don't panic, but your house is on fire."

Despite everyone's objections—his girlfriend, his daughter, his ex, his parents, and even his movie-star brother, Matt—Kevin went back. On the way, he passed the Point Dume shopping center. Parts of it were in flames, which meant the fire had crossed the highway. His favorite local bar in the center, the Duck Dive, looked to be in jeopardy. It was one thing for homes in the canyons and hills to burn but this was the largest commercial center in the city. Kevin thought maybe his family was right and that he should turn around, but he didn't.

David Ryan lived next door to Kevin and across the street from actor Nick Nolte. David had purchased the land in 2001 and built a rustic, Montana-farm-style home in 2010. The property had a small pool and a structure he called "the barn," which was really an extra-large storage shed, though it *was* painted red. David's son, Thomas, used the structure to shape and repair surfboards, a lucrative business for a young guy in Malibu.

Like Kevin, David had never lived through a fire before, but on a hunch, he'd bought twelve one-gallon containers of Barricade, a fire retardant that could be applied to his house with a garden hose. A few years earlier, he'd asked his father for an unusual Christmas gift—a fire pump. Like an ugly sweater, the pump had been sitting unused—and untested—in David's garage for years.

"Aren't you going to test that thing?" his wife kept asking. "You might want to know how to use it."

A few months before the fire, David and Thomas finally fired up the pump using the water from his pool. David realized he didn't have enough hose to spray Barricade on both his house and barn so he purchased another hundred feet.

On the Monday before the fire, David asked a contractor to give him a bid on the cost of installing a generator. In an earthquake—or a wildfire—a generator would be critical. His home had a well system, which he used to irrigate his plants, but the well had pumps that required electricity. He'd received a detailed proposal from the contractor on Wednesday. The next day, the Woolsey Fire began its march.

David had a meeting scheduled that Friday morning in Irvine, a two-hour drive down the coast. Because of the approaching fire, he asked to join the meeting via conference call. At 8:30, as his call was about to begin, the power went out. Worse than the missed meeting, David no longer had access to his well water.

Thomas had planned to drive down to San Diego for a surf contest scheduled for Saturday but decided it wasn't a good idea to leave. The men pulled the pump from the garage and set it up by the pool. They searched for spigots to attach garden hoses, but every spigot was connected to the well water. On David's entire property, only one spigot was connected to the city water system. The men strung together every hose they had to create a second way to fight the fire. Already, they could see a massive cloud of smoke coming their way.

At 10:52 a.m., they spotted flames in nearby Zuma Canyon. David kept thinking they'd see some firefighters but their street was deserted. He saw a firefighting plane overhead, just one, but it passed without making a drop.

Fifteen minutes later, help arrived in the form of their contractor.

Stuart McCallister had built their home. He had been out on a work call in the area when he got trapped by the gridlock on the PCH. With no escape, he decided to check on the Ryans. As he arrived, flames appeared on the mountain above them.

The three men began applying the Barricade gel to the house using David's two hoses. Thomas was operating the pool pump but he yanked too hard when starting the engine. The plastic handle cracked and the pull cord disappeared inside the pump.

Without the cord, they couldn't start the engine. The three men huddled over the machine. Without it, they were screwed. Fortunately, McCallister had a massive set of tools in his truck.

He grabbed a socket wrench set and began taking the pump apart. He reached the cord and pulled it out, then reattached the parts he'd taken off. Finally, he fixed the handle so the cord wouldn't slip out again. With a single pull, the pump roared to life.

They sprayed the front of the house, then moved anything that might burn onto the grass lawn. After they finished, David and Thomas drove to the base of Zuma Canyon, about a mile away, to check on the fire's progress. They parked in front of a house to assess the fire's path.

Two men, who appeared to be father and son, sprinted out from the driveway of the home.

"Who are you? What are you doing here?" the father shouted, visibly alarmed.

"Uh, we live down the street," said David. "We're checking on the fire."

The man seemed to relax slightly. "We've had looters try to rob us twice. One guy tried to steal my car while I was in the back. They're driving around on motorcycles with satchels on the side. Be careful."

When Kevin Dillon returned to Bonsall, it wasn't his house on fire; it was Nick Nolte's. In an odd twist of fate, Kevin's brother, Matt, was on location in Europe shooting a film with Nolte. Earlier that day, he'd pleaded with Kevin not to go back to save his house.

"What are you, an idiot?" Matt had said. "Get out of there."

Kevin wondered what his brother would think about him trying to save Nolte's place.

Enlisting the help of the returning Ryans, along with McCallister, Kevin and the men started spraying water all over Nolte's property, which bordered Zuma Creek. Propane tanks exploded around them causing Kevin to flinch and reminding him of his time on the set of *Platoon*—except these weren't special effects. They took turns shooting water into the dry creek, which was full of chaparral, through knot holes in Nolte's fence in an attempt to stop the embers from penetrating his property. Nolte's long row of pine trees went up in flames, their branches sounding like firecrackers as they snapped. Piles of wood from a remodeling project on his property also caught fire, as did a guest house built around a large sycamore tree. The men were fighting a raging inferno with nothing but a bunch of garden hoses. Kevin didn't even have a mask. None of the men had goggles or fire protection.

Kevin noticed flames coming from the home of his friend Susie, who lived next door to Nolte. He hurried to her property and found a storage container full of antique furniture on fire—but it was too late. He shoveled dirt on as many spot fires as he could so the fire wouldn't spread to her house. Then he remembered Susie's chicken coop.

He raced to the coop, which was about to ignite. He opened the pen to free the chickens, but they wouldn't move and stared at him in shock. Finally, he shooed them out. At least now they had the chance to flee.

With the chickens safe, he left Susie's property and spotted a fireman in a red SUV.

"Hey, I got a fire over here," he said, hustling over to the man. "I need help."

Kevin thought the fireman would call in an engine and perhaps Nolte's home could be saved. After all, the neighborhood still had water, which meant the engine could blast the home using the hydrants.

"Where? Where?" the fireman asked.

"Follow me." Kevin hurried toward Nolte's yard but when he turned back the SUV was driving away. That was the only firefighter he saw.

Kevin and the Ryans continued to try to save Nolte's home, until they noticed flames on the other side of the street—their side of the street. The fire had snuck down the creek bed and jumped to their homes. While Kevin's Mediterranean had stucco walls and a tile roof, which made it somewhat fire resistant, David's home was constructed of wood. One ember could burn down the entire structure. As they crossed the street, David's barn burst into flames. Ninety-foot tall palm trees exploded above them, showering them with embers. Even the tree trunks blazed with fire.

They began using the fire pump, but the hose wasn't long enough to reach the barn where the flames were most intense. With another ten feet, David could have saved it. The men watched, helpless, as the barn burned to the ground.

Kevin and the Ryans worked late into the night putting out spot fires.

"I was afraid to go to sleep," Kevin said. "I thought I'd wake up inside a burning house."

But he was also exhausted. His lungs ached from the smoke. Finally, he went to bed but set his alarm to go off every two hours. Each time he awoke, he walked the neighborhood and extinguished embers. At one point, Kevin saw an army of monster-sized rats tumbling down the hillside as they ran from the flames.

The next day brought more of the same. Kevin even went to my home on Saturday with Chris Wynne to put out spot fires from my railroad ties. While they were in my backyard, other locals stopped to assist them. A woman, Bridgette Fox, brought sandwiches for everyone. When I returned home after the evacuation, I thought the fire department had moved the railroad ties away from my home to keep it from burning. But Malibu locals had done that job, most of whom I didn't even know.

Throughout the ensuing days, Kevin and other neighbors gathered to make meals and keep each other company—and keep each other safe. Numerous looters were coming into the area. Fortunately, Kevin's neighbor on his other side was Tom Fakehany, a retired sheriff. Fakehany had stayed behind with his wife. He was also armed.

For Kevin, staying was one of the most rewarding experiences of his life. He felt proud that he and his newfound brothers had saved their homes.

"It was like a war," he said, a struggle the men had won. The efforts of Kevin, David, and the others prevented the spread of the fire to the rest of the neighborhood, as not a single house below them burned. He nicknamed David "Captain Ryan," for his efforts with the fire pump.

I imagined Kevin falling to his knees like Johnny Drama did in one of the most iconic moments from *Entourage* shouting, "Thank you God. Victory!" when he knew his home was safe.

By Monday, however, living in Malibu didn't feel like a win. Kevin's lungs were "jacked up" from the toxic soot and ash in the air. They would bother him for months. While everyone else in his family was okay—at least physically—many of their animals were not. Three died within weeks of the fire.

"Would you do it again?" I asked him.

He didn't hesitate. "A hundred percent," he said.

Kevin Dillon, Bridgette Fox, and other good samaritans who put out spot fires at my house.

PHOTO CHRIS WYNNE

Craig Conklin's crew sleeping on the beach to avoid the flames.
PHOTO CRAIG CONKLIN

18

SECRET SERVICE

Craig Conklin has been a Major League Baseball scout for nearly twenty years. For fifteen of those years, he worked for MLB's central scouting bureau preparing detailed reports on players. Since 2014, he has been employed as a part-time scout by the Oakland A's.

Because part-time scouting doesn't cover the bills, Craig has another job. His small security company, On Point Private Security, provides personal protection services for some of the most famous people in the world. Celebrities like Julia Roberts and Chris Martin of Coldplay hired Craig because he'd grown up in Malibu. They wanted a local they could trust. With his background as an Army Airborne Assault specialist, and later a firefighter and Emergency Medical Technician, Craig could handle himself in a variety of situations.

On the Friday of the fire, Craig was staying with his girlfriend, Jena, on the Central Coast when he received a phone call at 3:00 a.m.

"We're being evacuated," said his friend Ryan, who lived in the Agoura area. "Can I stay at your place in Malibu?"

"Of course," said Craig. "Take anything you need."

A few hours later, Ryan called again with the news that Malibu was now being evacuated. "What do you want me to get from your place?" he asked.

Craig had two daughters. The younger one, Jordan, had died in a car accident almost exactly a year earlier.

"Grab any picture of my kids." Those were the only items that mattered to him. Jordan's ashes were already in the center console of his Suburban, along with three locks of her hair. He'd been driving around with them for over a year, unsure what to do with them. "Throw them in my Oakland A's bag."

Craig knew he had to get back to Malibu. He had properties to protect but more importantly, people who were going to need him. He and Jena loaded up his Suburban, though it was more like they *overloaded* it. Jena packed as much food as possible, sensing it could become scarce in an emergency situation. They picked up his best friend, Brian Weissmann, on their way down the coast since Craig was going to need a wingman he could count on. Brian was also an employee of On Point Private Security.

Their first mission was to rescue an elderly couple Craig called his "surrogate parents." Doug and Dottie O'Brien were in their mid-eighties and lived adjacent to Kevin Dillon in the Bonsall neighborhood of Malibu. A former fireman, Doug was "one tough old bird," but the years of pulling heavy fire hose had left him barely able to walk.

When the group entered Malibu around one o'clock that Friday afternoon, Craig talked his way through the first checkpoint, but on the PCH at Encinal Canyon, the LA County sheriffs wouldn't let him pass. Beyond the checkpoint, fire on the hillsides extended as far as Craig could see.

"My parents are in there," he said. "They live off Bonsall. I've got to get them out."

"The fire is right there. It's not safe," said the sheriff in charge.

"I'm a former firefighter," Craig said. "I'm ex-military. I can take care of myself."

"Sorry, can't do it."

Craig locked eyes with the sheriff. "Come on, man, what if they were your parents?"

The sheriff glanced down the coastline and shook his head as if he couldn't believe he was considering letting them through. "You're taking your life in your hands." He turned and eyed Jena and Brian. "And your passengers' lives too."

"I promise I'll keep them safe," Craig said.

The sheriff scanned the vehicle again to make sure Jena and Brian understood the danger. When they nodded, he pointed at Craig. "It's all on you." He waved them through with a disgusted flick of his hand.

As the group neared the O'Brien property, the sky turned black, despite it being the afternoon. Flames coated the houses around them. Suddenly, flames surrounded the Suburban as well. Craig felt the heat from inside the car. He feared the electronics would fry, leaving them trapped in the vehicle. He gunned the engine and, somehow, they made it through without burning alive.

When they reached the O'Brien house, the fire was less than a hundred feet away. Across the street, flames claimed Nick Nolte's property. Craig and his friends dashed into Doug and Dottie's house.

"The fire's heading here now," said Craig. "We gotta go."

But the elderly couple didn't seem to understand the urgency of the situation. "I've been here for forty-six years," Doug said. "The fire never comes down this far."

"We're not leaving," said Dottie.

On the ride over, Craig had discussed with Jena and Brian how stubborn the couple could be, especially Doug. They agreed they would remove them no matter what, even if they were "kicking and screaming." But before Craig dragged them out of their own house, he decided to open the front door.

"Oh my gosh," said Dottie when she saw the flames on her property. "I had no idea."

Sensing there was a first for everything, including a catastrophic fire in his section of Bonsall Canyon, Doug gave in.

With no time for packing or further conversation, the group scooped Doug and Dottie up and hurried back to the car and raced toward Westward Beach. Craig wanted to make a run for it down the PCH to Santa Monica, but he was also afraid of being in a "stampede environment" should flames come over the highway in the neighborhoods that were already on fire. He knew the beach was the safest place to be so he drove to Grayfox Street on Point Dume.

At the beach gate, they encountered a woman with an eight-month-old baby, a two-year-old toddler, and a dog. Rachel had been evacuated from her nearby condo when the flames got too close.

Though all beaches in California are ostensibly public, access to those beaches is often not. Homeowners have installed a number of locked beach gates to prevent outsiders from getting to the trails which lead to Point Dume's world-famous surfing beaches.

Because of Craig's client base, he had access to many area properties—and beach keys. One client, Erik Swan, told him to "break a window" to enter his home, but Craig was reluctant to do so. His job was to protect his clients' properties, not trash them. He set his group up, which now included Rachel, her daughters, and her dog on the outdoor decks in Erik's backyard. They sat there for hours as it got dark. Jena acted as "Team Mom" and made sure the older people were comfortable on the lawn furniture. She unloaded food from the Suburban and kept everyone fed and safe, especially the children.

Craig and Brian regularly walked down Grayfox Street to see if the orange glow was dissipating—or getting brighter. But it was hard to tell. They ran into other neighbors who said the PCH was a "shit show." Jena wanted to get everyone away from the wooden decks of the house and down to the beach. Already it was past 9:00 p.m. She didn't want to fall asleep only to be awakened by nearby flames with no quick way to move two people in their mid-eighties, one of whom had trouble walking.

Craig and Brian began lugging the lawn furniture down the trail to set up camp on the sand. Craig and Jena pulled the remaining supplies out of his Suburban as well. They figured they might not see the vehicle again since it could be melted come morning.

"Aren't you forgetting something?" Jena asked.

It took him a second to remember that Jordan's ashes were in the vehicle, along with the locks of her hair. He imagined his daughter laughing at him for keeping her remains in the console of his SUV.

"What are you doing, you fool?" he heard her voice in his head. "You don't need my ashes to remember me."

But he hadn't been able to let go of them. Until now. In the air, ashes from burned homes drifted by him. Were people going to save those in a box too?

"I don't need them," he told Jena. "I don't need to carry them to carry her with me."

When they rejoined the others, Craig helped Doug down the trail, while Jena supported Dottie. Brian helped Rachel with her girls. On the sand, Craig discovered he still had cell service and called Chris Martin.

"Pillage whatever you need from my place," the rock star told him. "Anything you want—it's yours."

He and Brian gathered sleeping bags and comforters from Chris' house to keep everyone warm during the night ahead. They also grabbed two wetsuits and a two-person kayak. Worst-case scenario, if the flames blew down the creek and stormed onto the sand, Brian and Craig would throw on the wetsuits, put Doug and Dottie in the kayak, and wade into the ocean. Jena would take one child, Rachel the other. They, too, would go waist deep into the ocean to avoid the flames.

From the beach, Craig could see the fire moving toward Paradise Cove. He felt helpless and terrible for everyone near the blaze. Brian sat facing away from the ocean and toward the canyon searching for signs of fire activity coming their way. Periodically, one of them would go up the trail to check the street, always leaving the other behind to stand guard should there be an emergency. Craig described it as "the worst night" he'd ever had.

He finally succumbed to sleep, sporadic as it was. In the morning, when the group awoke, they were covered in ash. Trees on the cliffsides above them were black. The fire had burned as far as it possibly could.

Doug had been the first one up and wanted to leave. "I don't want to sit here," he said. "I'm going back."

"You can't," Craig said, "it's not safe."

The old man ignored him and hobbled toward the trail. "I'm going home."

"Jesus, okay, but let me go to your house first to make sure it's all right."

"Fine."

Craig got into his Suburban, which hadn't melted, and drove down Dume Drive. The homes of five of his friends were gone. Others were still ablaze. But the O'Brien home had survived.

He returned to the beach camp and began to pack everyone up. They loaded Doug and Dottie into their vehicle and followed Rachel and her kids to their condo complex, which miraculously, also still stood. After dropping the family off, they returned the O'Briens to their home, but the air quality was toxic and dangerously unsafe. Doug seemed to be suffering mentally as well.

"I'm going to get my car washed," he said.

That was his regular Saturday routine—driving over Kanan Dume Road to get his car cleaned—but this was no ordinary weekend, something Doug appeared to be struggling to understand.

"You can't go anywhere," Craig said. "The roads are closed."

Jena didn't think the couple should be left alone. They called Doug and Dottie's daughter, Kelly, and then drove them to her home in Santa Ynez, over two hours away.

After safely dropping them off, Craig switched from fire mode to security mode. Cinemaphotographer Danny Moder, Julia Roberts' husband, asked Craig to come back to Malibu and watch their house "until things settled down." Already, there were reports of looting. What home could be a bigger target than that of a major celebrity?

Craig and Brian headed to Malibu, this time without Jena. But they couldn't talk their way in this time. The authorities refused to let in anyone without proper credentials. Craig and Brian drove down every canyon road trying to find some path in. They ran into a friendly cop who wouldn't let them pass but clued them into a way they might be able to get through. A number of gated communities had opened their gates due to the emergency, which meant it was possible to drive through them to avoid certain checkpoints. The men drove through three such communities and when it looked like they'd found a way into Malibu, they heard a siren. Parked on the side of the road was a lone cop manning a checkpoint.

Craig glanced at Brian, who nodded, and Craig hit the gas. He gambled the cop wouldn't abandon his post to chase after him. While he was right, the road was treacherous and filled with downed power poles and fallen trees. More than once, they had to get out and move objects out of the road.

For the next week, Craig stood guard inside Julia Roberts' gates. At night, he slept in his Suburban with the windows down so he could hear if anything was amiss. Brian did the same at Chris Martin's property. During the day, the men raked leaves, swept porches and driveways, washed cars—anything to make the homes appear lived in. Without power in Malibu, all of the alarm systems and cameras were out, so it was back to old-fashioned ways of fooling robbers and looters.

One afternoon, while Craig was checking on a friend, Brian took a shift guarding Julia's place. He was raking leaves on her driveway when a red fire department utility vehicle with Colorado license plates pulled up. Two men wearing firefighting outfits were inside but only one got out. The man approached Brian, asking him to confirm the property's address. Brian had learned to question everyone's actions and motives when guarding celebrities. Even things that looked legitimate often were not. Paparazzi disguised themselves as surfers to get pictures, carrying telephoto lenses in backpacks. Recently, Julia and Danny had remodeled part of their home and put some furniture in storage. Days later, the tabloids published that their marriage was over and Danny was moving out. Because of incidents like these, Brian kept his mouth shut around anyone he didn't know.

When he didn't give up the address, the man said, "We've been sent on behalf of the insurance company to verify their client is fine and that nothing is damaged. Is this where J. Roberts lives?"

While everything about the man's outfit (and vehicle) said firefighter, the nature of the visit didn't seem "legit." Brian knew that tabloids like TMZ weren't above bribery to get what they wanted. The only individuals getting through in all situations and circumstances were those in the fire department.

"What's the big deal with a couple of photos?" he imagined the tabloids saying to the firefighter in front of him. "We all gotta make money. Work with us. If you get us some shots, we'll get you good money."

Brian felt badly doubting the integrity of a (possible) firefighter, but the man had offered no ID or even a card from the supposed insurance company. The guy didn't even know Julia's address.

"We need to take pictures of the property," the man continued. "And the family."

Brian had heard enough. "It's not going to happen."

The man looked discouraged and hung his head, as if he'd blown his big payday. "I see."

"Nobody is getting on this property. You need to move on. Right now."

The man went back to the vehicle, but the driver didn't start the car. Brian was uneasy about the standoff. Typically, those looking for photos waited for an opportunity to sneak through an open gate or to jump over a fence. Finally, the men did a slow loop in front of the house and drove off.

The Friday after the fire, Brian and Craig were driving around Point Dume on Chris Martin's golf cart looking for similar odd behavior. They spotted several black sedans and a fire utility vehicle parked on Wandermere Street on the remains of a burned home. Craig assumed it was the grief-stricken family and a fire official in his dress whites. But the earlier experience at Julia's house had put Brian on edge.

"Hey, who are you guys? Do you have a right to be here?" he asked.

The fire official came over. "They're Secret Service. They're trying to find a route for the President."

Craig overheard the agents, who wore black shirts and tan khaki pants, discussing the safest route in and out of the neighborhood, which still gave some sense of the fire damage.

"Well, the best way is Dume Drive," said Craig. "Second-worst hit street too."

One of the agents approached to talk with him. It turned out he was the site coordinator for the Secret Service, and in charge of logistics for the President's visit.

Craig filled him in on the neighborhood he knew so well. When the agents drove over to Dume Drive to verify Craig's intel, he and Brian followed in the golf cart.

The group parked in the driveway of Richard Gibbs, the former keyboard player for Oingo Boingo. Gibbs' home had been destroyed, but his Woodshed Recording Studio, which had hosted the likes of U2, Barbra Streisand, Lady Gaga, Pink, Lorde, and Coldplay was untouched.

Craig and Brian thought it disrespectful that the agents were traipsing onto people's property without permission. Gibbs hadn't even been back to go through the rubble of his home and now strangers, including members of the White House press corps, were walking anywhere they wanted. They were also concerned that published pictures of the Woodshed Studio might alert looters to the expensive equipment sitting unprotected inside.

"What's the nature of your business here?" Brian asked.

"We're FEMA," said one of the men. Others were Secret Service, he added.

"Yeah, but what gives you the right to come onto this property?"

"We're FEMA," repeated the man as though that fact gave him the right, which it probably did.

Brian and Craig were dressed in black with sweatshirts that identified them as private security. The agents and FEMA reps likely assumed they were responsible for Gibbs' property and gave Brian some latitude as he continued to question them.

"You told me who you are," he said. "I'm asking why you're here."

"I just told you. We're FEMA."

"I'm going to have to ask you to step off this property."

By now the FEMA rep had had enough of Brian and approached one of the Secret Service agents. "This guy's a little agitated," he told them. "He's getting kind of aggressive."

Fortunately, Craig overheard the conversation and pulled Brian by the back of his shirt, ushering him away before the Secret Service arrested him. Shortly thereafter, however, the agents and FEMA reps moved off the Gibbs property and onto the street. Brian's message about showing the locals some respect had gotten through.

The next afternoon, November 17, Craig and Brian were making the rounds when they noticed the same group set up in the area. The site coordinator came over to thank Craig for his assistance the day before and introduced himself as Sean. As they spoke, the Secret Service began to set up for President Trump's arrival. Craig saw German shepherds and guys with long sniper rifles. But after Sean moved on, no one bothered Craig or Brian. They'd gained credibility by talking with the site coordinator. So they stood there, watching, as assets were put in place to protect the President of the United States. One agent even asked them, "Are you guys staging here too?"

Craig figured, fuck it, if we're going to impersonate Secret Service agents, we might as well act like we're part of the team. "Yeah, until Sean tells us to move."

"I hear that," said the agent.

Craig and the agent discussed possible vulnerable points on the route while they waited for the Presidential motorcade. When it arrived, Craig and Brian were feet away. During the press briefing, the President mentioned the town he'd come from in Northern California, a town obliterated by the Camp Fire.

"What we saw at Pleasure," the President began, as officials standing next to him—Governor Jerry Brown, Governor-elect Gavin Newsom, FEMA Administrator Brock Long, Fire Chief Daryl Osby, and others—seemed to cringe. The only one who had the courage to correct him was a reporter named Jennifer.

"Paradise," she said.

"We just left Pleasure," Trump chattered on obliviously. But the others on stage with him couldn't let the grievous error pass twice. Eighty people had died in that town. At least, the President could get the name right.

"Paradise," the men on stage said in unison.

Trump kept going as if he'd said the name right all along.

Malibu local prepared to defend against looters

PHOTO JONNY PALMER

Mudslide in my Malibu Park neighborhood

PHOTO ROBERT KERBECK

19

COOL HAND MIKKE

Mikke Pierson was elected to the Malibu City Council three days before the Woolsey Fire, so he wasn't yet officially in office when the blaze took place.

That didn't stop him from taking charge.

Like practically everyone who grew up in Malibu, Mikke is a surfer, though his soul patch makes him look more like a beatnik poet. He is also the son of Hollywood royalty. His father, Frank, was a director and the writer of such iconic films as *Cool Hand Luke* and *Dog Day Afternoon*.

After heading north to attend UC Santa Cruz and try out some different waves, Mikke returned to Malibu to work at the surf shop of another city council member, Jefferson "Zuma Jay" Wagner. Mikke and Jefferson became partners and opened a store in Santa Monica. I bought my first surfboard there in 1993.

On the day of our February 2 interview, which occurred at Malibu City Hall during a flash flood *and* mud slide warning, our cell phones rang at the same moment with the sound of blasting alarms warning us to take immediate action for our safety.

I was interviewing Mikke *about* a disaster *during* a disaster.

Mudslides, also known as debris avalanches, are a type of landslide that often occurs after wildfires. Since the flames consume all the vegetation that protects the soil, nothing is left to hold it in place. After a fire, the ground is charred, creating a hard layer on top of it, resulting in a hydrophobic effect where, rather than absorbing water, the soil *repels* it. Rains skim down hillsides and slopes, picking up speed, boulders, and the remains of homes along the way.

Mikke was supposed to give me thirty minutes, but given what was going on, I would've understood if he'd cancelled the whole thing. Instead, he gave me two and a half hours, though he took frequent breaks to check his phone for texts and emails. He received a panicked call from his wife, Maggie, about the flooding in his Malibu West neighborhood. She'd just come from pounding on the door of one of her neighbors, warning them to evacuate. That neighbor, Damon Skelton, happened to be one of my surfer buddies and a good friend.

While numerous locals had stayed behind to fight the fire, no one would stay behind to fight a mudslide. Once the mud starts flowing, no one can stop it. After the 2017 Thomas Fire in nearby Ventura and Santa Barbara Counties, twenty-one people died in the mudslides in Montecito. Only two had died in the fire itself.

"Get out," Maggie yelled when Damon opened the door. "Get out now!"

Damon's seven-year-old son was playing naked. His wife was in bed with a herniated disc. His daughter was in her pajamas. Fortunately, they'd only half-unpacked from the fire evacuation, so Damon threw some things back into the suitcases and helped his son get dressed. He carried the kids and suitcases to his SUV, which was surrounded by swirling brown water and three feet of mud but, because of Maggie's early warning, they'd gotten out in time to avoid being stuck.

The Malibu West community is the Mayberry of Malibu. The houses are closer together than in the rest of the city. The neighborhood has sidewalks, block parties, and an HOA. Kids tear down the flat streets on bikes and skateboards. Though Malibu West adjoins my Malibu Park neighborhood, it is the former that is more like a park. The communities couldn't be more different. As one example, I was petrified anytime my son went bike riding on the steep hills and blind curves of Malibu Park and, after a couple of crashes, including one in which he broke both his arms, I forbid it altogether. For another, no one would knock on my door to warn me about a mudslide.

Over the continued clangs on our phones, Mikke said that, on the day of the Woolsey Fire, he'd been up since 2:00 a.m. Like many locals, he was studying the weather and wind reports. He had a sick feeling the fire was coming their way. He and his twenty-three-year-old son, Emmet, decided to stay behind to fight it. Emmett was 6'2", worked out six days a week, and was into all things military. Before going into commercial real estate, he had considered becoming a Navy SEAL.

"We're not going to be heroes," Mikke told Maggie to assuage her fears. "I promise."

Maggie and their daughter, Gracie, left at 8:00 a.m. to evacuate down the PCH toward Santa Monica when everyone else in Malibu was doing the same thing. Inexplicably, those in charge of the roads hadn't considered the huge numbers of people leaving at the same time.

Maggie tried to detour through the Point Dume area but too many people were doing the same thing. She and Gracie were trapped. Mikke told her to head to the parking lot at Zuma Beach. Worst case scenario, they could go to the sand, which wasn't going to burn, or wade into the water at the ocean's edge.

That call would be the last time they spoke for twelve hours.

At 10:00 a.m., Mikke and Emmet drove to the end of Paseo Canyon Road at the base of Trancas Canyon. They watched as the fire picked up speed and began blasting down the Santa Monica Mountains. Mikke called it his "oh shit" moment. Not only would he and his son be fighting a fire, it was far bigger than he'd expected.

Mikke was prepared, however, in a way that most people, even others who stayed like me, were not. He and Emmet had fire helmets, goggles, masks, thick gloves, and turnout coats similar to those worn by firefighters, which provided mobility and breathability while protecting against burn injuries. Unlike other locals with their make-shift gear, Mikke and Emmett looked like firefighters, though their gear didn't have any insignias.

As the fire poured into Malibu West, a handful of neighbors stayed behind, including Tim Biglow, David Meyers, Dermot Stoker, and Jordan Clarke. The men focused their efforts on the homes closest to the mountains. If any of those caught fire, it would create a domino effect throughout the neighborhood of 237 residences.

Mikke wasn't worried about his own home, which was lower down from the mountains and had a metal roof, no vents, and good brush clearance. Using garden hoses, Mikke, Emmet, and the others patrolled the neighborhood on foot, putting out embers and spot fires before they got out of control. Unlike my Malibu Park neighborhood, which lost water and went dry around noon, Malibu West continued to have water. Their tank was higher than the homes in the neighborhood so the water was gravity-fed.

To cover more ground and save more houses, the men split up. Mikke recalled putting out fires at one home, which didn't have a hose, with a water wand device used to water plants.

Mikke didn't run into his first professional firefighter until 2:00 p.m., despite the fact that the fire had been raging in Malibu West for hours. An engine from San Diego was parked further down Paseo Canyon Road, far from where the action—and fire damage—was taking place.

In fact, where the engine was, not a single fire burned.

"I'm by myself," Mikke told the firefighters. "I'm losing homes. I could use your help up at the base of the canyon."

"We can't go up a box canyon," said the captain, referring to a type of canyon with a single access point and steep walls on all sides. "I won't be able to turn my engine around."

"It's not a box canyon," Mikke explained. "There's plenty of room for you guys to turn around."

"Sorry, it's not safe."

"Well, as soon as you figure out how to drive 200 yards straight up this road, my son and I will be up there saving houses."

One could argue that the firefighters weren't passing on saving lives, only homes. But, Mikke wondered, wasn't that what firefighters were supposed to do? Protect lives *and* property? If they were so worried about getting their engine stuck, why didn't they leave it and walk the 200 yards to assess the situation. It's not like they were going to get incinerated walking up the streets of Malibu West. They had more protective gear and clothing than Mikke and the others did. Plus, Malibu West had water, so the firefighters didn't even need the 500 gallons their engine carried. Why had they signed up to be firefighters if they weren't going to fight the blaze?

Due to the efforts of Mikke, Emmet, and others, Malibu West lost only twenty-one out of 237 homes and condominiums. Mikke believed he could have saved all but a few homes if he had the help of a couple of more people—or firefighters. During our interview, he played a video that showed the home of the Malibu school principal, Pat Cairns, going up in flames. In the background, Mikke was crying.

"I'm so sorry, Pat. I tried. I tried."

Around six o'clock in the evening, once the initial firestorm had passed through Malibu West, Mikke drove over to Point Dume to help Tim Biglow save his father's home. The fire was hitting Dume just as it was getting dark, adding drama to a situation that didn't need any more of it. On Dume Drive, it seemed every home was on fire. Again, Mikke didn't see a single firefighter.

At Tim's father's house, the fire was "gnarly." There were three garden hoses but only enough pressure to use one at a time. At one point, an explosion from the collapse of a nearby home shot thousands of embers into the air. Mikke decided it was too dangerous, but Tim wouldn't leave.

As Mikke drove out of the neighborhood, he likened the scene to a sci-fi movie right after the aliens zap the planet. As he drove by the Pavilions market on Point Dume, his phone, which had been quiet all day due to the lack of service, went berserk. By the time it stopped dinging and donging, he had over fifty voicemails and 200 texts, including nineteen from his wife, who feared he had died.

He went back to check on Tim, who was not only alive but had saved his father's home.

"How the hell did you do that?" Mikke asked.

Tim said that whenever he got in trouble, he turned the hose on himself.

At their home in Malibu West, Mikke and Emmet fell asleep around two o'clock in the morning while watching a house go up in flames on nearby Tapia Drive. They were just too exhausted to do anything about it.

In the morning, they woke to find a house they'd saved the day before now burning down. They grabbed a sheriff to get a fire engine, which came and saved two other houses. Mikke hollered, "Better late than never."

As they walked through the neighborhood, looking for hot spots to put out, saving three more homes along the way, a ninety-year-old woman came out from one of the homes. She was in a robe and walking with a cane. No one even knew she was there.

In the days immediately after the fire, when the mandatory evacuation was still in place, Mikke made it his mission to inform those who had lost their homes. He figured, what was eating people up was not knowing. He drove around the neighborhoods taking pictures of the burned homes, along with their addresses, then found a way to contact the person, usually via social media. Mikke estimated he told over a hundred people that they'd lost their homes.

Other missions included checking on animals that were lost or left behind. Kaliko Orian, owner of Kaliko Farms, asked him to get water to her brood of 1,000 chickens on Kanan Dume Road.

Along with two friends (one of whom was Bridgette Fox, the woman who fed Kevin Dillon and the other locals putting out spot fires in my backyard), Mikke tried to drive up Kanan, but he was stopped by a sheriff's roadblock. Mikke was wearing a red emergency vest with a city of Malibu logo. He flicked his Subaru's hazards on as if they were lights on a squad car.

"I need to get water to some chickens," he said.

The sheriff glowered at him as if she'd heard better excuses that day. The sheriffs had gotten a lot tougher in the days after the fire when people first started sneaking in. In the beginning, the closures had been "soft," which meant if you had a logical reason—you forgot your medicine or were bringing something to someone in need—a sympathetic sheriff might check your ID (and double check your story) before letting you pass.

But the closures had turned "hard" after a picture of armed vigilantes went viral on social media. Rumors of heavy looting had caused many locals to arm themselves. The picture showed a group of mostly masked men carrying rifles and long guns with a spray-painted sign threatening to shoot looters on sight, though the men had spelled it "site."

The last thing the sheriffs wanted was young men taking the law into their own hands, something the "Queen of Malibu," Mae Rindge, had done in the early 1900s. The policy of her guards was to shoot first and ask questions later whenever they encountered anyone on her 13,000-acre Rancho Malibu property. One could argue the men on Point Dume were simply following a long-standing Malibu tradition.

"We're not letting anyone in," said the sheriff.

"But I'm saving baby chickens," Mikke said, hoping to appeal to the animal lover in her.

She shrugged. "Not happening."

"I'm a city council person."

"You're not getting in."

Technically, though, Mikke wanted to get *out* of Malibu. Most of the sheriffs operating the roadblocks weren't from the area and had little knowledge of the geography. Often, the stops were set in places where there were ways around them, which, of course, the locals used to their advantage. But the hard stops had begun to sour the community on the very people sworn to protect them. The hostile attitudes of many sheriffs didn't help.

Finally, like an actor in one of his father's famous movies, Mikke gave it everything he had, "My house burned down."

He figured that would make the sheriff take pity and cut him—and the chickens—a break.

"Sorry to hear that," the sheriff said unsympathetically, "but I still can't let you in."

"No matter what you say, I'm going up there. It's my mission to save those chickens."

"I'll arrest you."

"Really? Are we there?"

"Yes, we're there."

Mikke inched his Subaru forward, indicating he was going to blow through the checkpoint, but the sheriff moved in front of the vehicle to block him.

"I'm going to find a way in," he shouted out his window. "You're not going to stop me."

"Have you not heard anything I've said?" the sheriff asked.

"Then I'm going to come back here and tell you about it."

"And I'm going to arrest you."

Mikke made a U-turn and tried to peel out but the Subaru was only a four cylinder. He found a route to the chicken farm which was longer and required that he and his friends walk part of the way. When they finally got there, a mass of hungry, thirsty, and panicked chickens swarmed them. They found feed for the birds but no water. They'd brought water with them in a couple of five-gallon containers, but it was far from enough. They gave the chickens the water in their water bottles too.

Desperate to find more water, they went from house to house, putting out hotspots along the way. Finally, at the fifth or sixth house, Bridgette found hoses that worked. She'd started filling their water containers when a man came out onto the deck of the home.

"What the hell are you doing?" He was shirtless and wearing boxer shorts. From the tone of his voice, it sounded like he thought they were looters. (With the cost of water in California and the amount the chickens were going to need, they were, in a sense, stealing.)

"I'm so sorry," said Bridgette. "We need water for chickens."

The guy glared down at them. Right when it looked like he might go inside and grab a shotgun, he said, "You need more jugs, take mine. Just make sure to bring them back."

"Thank you, dude!"

The group filled countless containers of water and the chickens drank them dry. They had to make multiple trips to the guy's home.

Who knew chickens could drink so much water? Mikke thought.

In the process of lugging the heavy water containers, he threw his back out. He'd fought a wildfire, climbing on roofs to do so, but it was the chickens that injured him.

Later, Mikke and Bridgette drove to the checkpoint at Kanan and the PCH. The same female sheriff was still on duty.

"Don't do it," Bridgette said.

Mikke, hazards flashing, hopped out of his car.

"I fed those chickens!" Mikke yelled like he was Paul Newman in *Cool Hand Luke* and daring the sheriff to shoot him. "And I'll be back tomorrow."

The sheriff looked at him with contempt. But she didn't do a thing.

Burned mobile homes in the Point Dume Club.
The neighborhood was saved by firefighters.

PHOTO ROBERT KERBECK

20

PRISON CAMP 13

I wanted to speak with LA County Fire Captain Chris Hanson because he grew up in Malibu. Ironically, he is friends with my surf buddy Tim, who was the first to warn me about firefighters not showing up. I hoped Chris could help me understand the radically different points of view on the efforts of the fire department during the Woolsey Fire.

On one side, there were residents who saw little to no effort to save homes. Malibu City Manager Reva Feldman, herself a lightning rod for criticism, said she was "shocked" by the stories of firefighters sitting in their engines refusing to engage or, worse, driving away from homeowners begging for help. On the other hand, the fire department said that this was a "one percent fire," unprecedented in size and scope, and that they did the best they could with the limited resources they had due to the fire up north in Paradise.

Three months after the fire, Chris picked me up on a Saturday morning in a red fire utility vehicle. Because it was so high off the ground, I had trouble climbing up. Chris slid easily into the driver's seat, while I had to latch onto the grab bar to hoist myself in.

With a voice like a growl, Chris sounds like he has sand from Zuma Beach permanently embedded in his throat. With his blonde hair, stocky build, and slightly sun-burned skin, he looks like a burly surfer. He acknowledged November 9 had been a tough day for the department, but he wanted to prove that firefighters hadn't just been sitting on their asses.

"I'm getting a lot of fuck yous," Chris said as we started off. "You never know who's going to throw a rock through your window. It's hurtful."

Signs abounded on the roads and fences of Malibu. They read:

Thank You to All Those Who Fought the Fires

To Everyone Involved, Thank You

The signs conspicuously did not mention, let alone praise, firefighters. Residents were angry at the number of homes lost. Their fury was compounded when the fire department initially bragged about what a great job they'd done.

The first place Chris wanted to show me was Camp 13, a female inmate camp high in the chaparral-filled hills of Malibu's Decker Canyon. The facility is the only all-female LA County Fire Department camp. Inmates there worked under firefighter supervision to assist with fire suppression. This meant cutting back years of overgrown brush with hand tools. In exchange, the nonviolent felons got fresh air, no prison bars, and better food. The camp had approximately fifty-five inmates along with ten Department of Corrections staff.

As we headed up steep Encinal Canyon Road to get to the camp, Chris told me his story of what had happened the Friday of the fire. That morning at 9:30, he and his son Hunter, also a firefighter, headed up to the camp with orders to protect it. As they drove, thick columns of smoke were visible. At first, Chris wasn't concerned, but as he and his son got closer, they spotted fire on the ridgeline above the camp. When they pulled in, they were surrounded by flames on all sides. Rivers of ash and sparks flew by, a phenomenon called ember wash—except he'd never seen it this bad. Engine 132 and Patrol 144 were already on scene with five or six firefighters. Chris said the firefighters had pre-staged at the camp, using the more aggressive firefighting strategy of prep-and-defend, which involved setting engines and men in front of the fire to knock it down. The firestorm was coming through when Chris and his son arrived, which meant that those present were taking on the worst of the Woolsey Fire.

It sounded like one hell of a rescue story and I was surprised I hadn't heard it before. But then Chris explained that the inmates had been evacuated a half-hour before he arrived.

"We got the girls out," he said. "They're trained but not for this."

The inmates, along with the staff, were already down at Zuma Beach.

Why then had Chris and his son come up to the camp? Why were an engine, patrol, and firefighters stationed there if they had no lives to protect? Why was the department using prep-and-defend high up in dangerous Decker Canyon when they didn't do so down in mostly flat neighborhoods like Point Dume or Malibu West?

In those neighborhoods (and most others), firefighters seemed to be letting the fire come through *first* in a technique known as fire front following. After the firestorm passes, firefighters go in to put out spot fires. The problem with that technique, of course, is that many homes are already gone by then.

When Chris and I pulled into Camp 13, I saw nothing worth saving. The facility's series of beige buildings looked like a run-down summer camp from the 1970s. A significant amount of brush surrounded the camp, including towering pine trees, which surprised me. I didn't understand why the inmates—or the fire department—hadn't cleared the highly flammable trees ages ago.

Chris walked me around the camp, describing the intense heat (and beating) the men had taken as the fire closed in on them from both sides.

"I've never seen a fire like this," he said. "This was a different level of experience."

Chris said one firefighter told him, "I'm scared."

With the seventy-mile-an-hour winds pelting them with embers continuously, even Chris got nervous. He started looking for a place to hide if flames overran them. Fortunately, the firefighters got control of the situation, though Chris lamented the loss of one dorm and a couple of outbuildings. "A bummer," he said.

With Camp 13 saved (for the most part), Chris and his son started down Encinal Canyon to "get back in the game." But by then the roads were inaccessible. It seemed like every power pole had come down. Power lines littered the streets. He described the scene as "apocalyptic." Because Chris was a local, however, he knew every side road. He tried multiple routes, even using his chainsaw to cut trees out of the road, but he couldn't find a path out of the canyon.

He and his son were stuck up there.

Chris spotted a resident in a car crossing over a power line, something firefighters were trained never to do. While Southern California Edison had shut off the power, no one without proper training and equipment could tell whether a line might still be energized.

Chris followed suit and crossed over the line. When he and his son didn't get electrocuted, they headed toward the beach.

"In my thirty years on the job, I've never run over wires," Chris said. "And I probably won't ever do it again."

When the tour of Camp 13 was over, Chris wanted to take me to the Point Dume Club, but while we were in Decker Canyon, I wanted to see Camp Kilpatrick.

Chris was more than accommodating and drove me to Kilpatrick, a ten-minute drive away. The facility was as different from Camp 13 as possible. Every building was new. There were basketball and volleyball courts. A pool. It looked like a small college campus.

Except there were no people.

Chris and I drove around the deserted facility where on the day of the fire Bruce Bates had driven out a van of kids as the fire closed in. Tanesha Lockhart had kept the rest safe when Fire Captain (and Malibu City Council Member) Rick Mullin ordered the kids and staff to shelter in place. Unlike Camp 13, however, Campus Kilpatrick seemed to be more defensible with lots of grass and a huge asphalt parking lot. The buildings, because they were new, were likely to be far more fire-resistant than the all-wood structures at Camp 13.

As Chris and I circled the camp, a woman came out from one of the buildings and introduced herself as Tammy. She explained that the camp was closed, though not from any damage from the fire, but rather the mudslides that followed it.

Afterwards, Chris took me to the Point Dume Club, a mobile home park approximately two miles from the one in Paradise Cove. He showed me the remains of three trailers, explaining that two LA County fire engines had stopped the fire from spreading to any of the other approximately 230 trailers in the community.

"It was a good save," he said. "A lot of the Dume Club could be gone."

He drove me to the Point Dume Plaza shopping center. The Friday of the Woolsey Fire, the post office there had caught fire. Engines put the fire out and saved the rest of the complex, one of the largest commercial centers in the city.

Chris implored me to "tell the good stuff" firefighters did that day. He said he'd been "spitting black" for two days afterwards. I could see his pain when he talked about how his department was being perceived in his own hometown. He practically winced each time he spoke.

I assured him I would—but I couldn't help wondering why Chris had risked his life, and that of his son, for a beat-up prison camp in one of the most dangerous parts of the Santa Monica Mountains during the height of the Woolsey Fire. Why had firefighter resources been pre-staged at Camp 13 and not at shiny new Campus Kilpatrick or in any Malibu neighborhood? Why was the prep-and-defend strategy used at Camp 13 and nowhere else in Malibu? Was the fire department more invested in protecting their own assets than those of homeowners?

"We do protect our properties," Chris told me when I asked him those questions. "We engaged where we thought we could do the most good. We never expected the fire was going to be this bad."

Referring to all the lost homes, Chris said, "It sucks, but we're not superhuman."

I understood this, as did every Malibu local I interviewed. We didn't expect miracles in the face of a fire as massive as Woolsey. We wanted to know that firefighters would come to our aid and not turn away. That firefighters would offer a hand—and a ladder—to save our homes. That firefighters had our backs and not just their own.

My neighbor in front of a massive
Eucalyptus tree toppled by the hurricane force winds

PHOTO ROBERT KERBECK

21

FIRE CHIEF IN THE HOT SEAT

Two and a half months after the Woolsey Fire, the city of Malibu hosted a town hall with the LA County Fire Department in an attempt to rebuild trust in the community since so many residents had lost homes. At the request of Malibu City Manager Reva Feldman, the leaders of the fire department showed up to explain that they hadn't failed residents. Far from it, they said. Fire Chief Daryl Osby believed the decision to order a mandatory evacuation of the city and surrounding areas had saved lives. But because the order was given for all areas at the exact same time, however, the Pacific Coast Highway—the only way out of Malibu—was instantaneously gridlocked. In the Camp Fire up north, the residents of Paradise had followed similar mass evacuation orders, jam-packing their one way out. When flames overtook the paralyzed road, dozens of people burned to death in their cars.

Rather than opening both, or at least one, of the PCH's Northbound lanes for Southbound traffic, the authorities had done nothing to alleviate the traffic nightmare—and potential death trap—of tens of thousands of people stuck in their vehicles as a monstrous wildfire approached. The authorities had also neglected to inform the public that the road northbound to Oxnard was open.

Many people mistakenly assumed the PCH was closed in that direction since the fire was coming from that way. As a result, the highway was clogged from Point Dume to Santa Monica, a span of over twenty miles.

Malibu City Council member Laura Rosenthal had people calling her from their cars, afraid they were going to be burned alive. Homeowners along the coast unlocked their gates so people could flee their vehicles and run to the beach if flames burned over the PCH, something that has happened in past fires. Pepperdine University, too, had issues with an evacuation of so many people at the same time, part of the reason they issued a shelter-in-place order for their students. Even though the campus was in the direct path of the fire, they believed it safer than a gridlocked Pacific Coast Highway.

Residents at the town hall might have been more willing to listen to Osby if the fire department wasn't also hosting a "honk the horn" event for children in the same location on the same day. It was a classic case of bureaucrats not considering how it might look, let alone feel, for residents to see children climbing in and out of shiny fire engines, the same engines so few people saw the day of the fire. People who'd lost their homes were arriving to find children ringing bells and honking horns, as if in celebration of that fact. No one in the fire department or the city manager's office seemed to anticipate the effect this would have. The event should have been moved elsewhere or, better yet, rescheduled to a different day—perhaps way down the road when the firefighters had reestablished trust with the community they swore to protect.

I wasn't surprised when the standing-room-only crowd began to verbally accost Osby and his team. In an attempt to calm the audience, the fire department played a video of the timeline of the fire to demonstrate how quickly it spread. Osby reminded the audience that the Woolsey Fire had burned nearly 100,000 acres and was the largest wildfire since LA County started keeping track. He talked about the extreme drought in California over the last few years. He detailed the lack of available resources due to the fire in Paradise, explaining he didn't get the out-of-state resources he needed until Sunday, day three of the fire. By then, most homes in jeopardy had already burned to the ground.

But residents like me already understood and had accepted all this. Most of the crowd was older and had been through fires before, some many times. While they were disappointed there weren't more firefighters, they also knew how terrible the situation was in Paradise where more than eighty people had died. What broke the hearts of residents like Patti Mehring and Paul Morra were the reports of firefighters standing by when homes could have been saved. Many in the audience had experienced this firsthand.

Osby claimed the fire department had no knowledge of this, which drove the crowd into a frenzy. He retreated to his refrain about the severity of the fire. He explained how the firefighting super scooper planes were grounded due to the winds, which hit seventy miles per hour, double the maximum the planes could handle. He had a Firehawk helicopter pilot, Mike Sagely, come up to address the challenge of the extreme conditions, but no one was disputing the danger or the size of the Woolsey Fire. Most in attendance had seen the fourteen-mile-long wall of flames along the PCH. What they wanted to know was why fire engines were sitting idly by the side of the road or refusing to go into neighborhoods.

But there were no answers that day. Osby and his team insisted they had no reports of this behavior—despite new city council member Mikke Pierson meeting in private with Osby for an hour *before* the meeting. Pierson had seen firefighters refusing to engage back in Malibu West and told Osby what he experienced, so Osby had at least one report—from an elected official.

I wasn't sure why the fire leaders kept denying what so many had personally observed, but I was going to find out.

It wasn't that Deputy Fire Chief Vince Pena didn't *want to* speak with me, it was more like he was *afraid to*. In his mind, LA County Fire had gotten a lot of bad press after the fire, which seemed to genuinely surprise him. He especially felt the *Los Angeles Times* had been unfair to the department, and because I'd had an Op-Ed in the paper, Pena considered me a part of the fourth estate—and hence a potential enemy. If it weren't for the introduction by my Malibu Park neighbor, retired Battalion Chief Berl Dahlstrom, who happened to be Pena's first training captain, I'm sure my emails requesting an interview would have been ignored. Indeed, my first ones were. It wasn't until I put "Berl Dahlstrom says hi" in the subject line that Pena called me.

Before he could meet with me, however, I had to email his boss, Fire Chief Osby, to clarify the purpose of my book. When I didn't hear anything back, I figured I had his permission and drove to the North Regional Operations Bureau in Santa Clarita to meet with Pena.

On the day I arrived, Pena was running late at an off-site meeting. His assistant, Lisa, showed me to a conference room where three large, colorful maps sat on a table. She offered me water or coffee, which I declined, then left me to wait for Pena.

The first map was of the homes lost in what was labeled the "Woolsey Incident." Little red dots indicated the homes that were destroyed. A lighter shade of red was used for those damaged. Dots littered the map. As I suspected, my Malibu Park neighborhood was hit the hardest, though there were many devastated areas: Decker Canyon, Latigo, Corral, Point Dume, to name a few.

A second map detailed the progression of the fire as it marched from the inception site, the Santa Susana Field Laboratory in Simi Valley, some thirty miles to the Pacific Ocean. Listed on the map were the times the fire arrived at key neighborhoods and communities along the way, making it clear how quickly the fire had traveled once it crossed the 101 Freeway.

While I found both maps illuminating (and heartbreaking), it was the map of past fires that was most informative. I already had a good sense of the number of homes lost since I drove by them every day. Each morning when I looked out my windows, I could see the remains of neighbor's homes, many of which I'd been inside. I also knew how fast the fire moved from firsthand experience. I had spotted flames coming over the horizon at 11:16 a.m. that Friday morning. Within minutes, the fire was burning homes half a mile away.

The historical map used different colors to show the areas that had burned in fires over the past thirty years. For the Woolsey Fire, the color was purple. The entire map seemed to be that color. Other large fires like the '93 Old

Topanga Fire seemed dwarfed in comparison. I knew the Woolsey Fire had burned 100,000 acres but it was something else to see it on a map. The fire had basically consumed all of western Malibu from the freeway to the ocean. The fire even bumped into one of the tunnels on Malibu Canyon Road in an attempt to cross into eastern Malibu and Topanga.

Pena arrived twenty minutes late and apologized for the delay. He has gentle brown eyes, thinning black hair, and like most firefighters, a bushy mustache. I was grateful for the time alone since the maps gave me perspective for what Pena had described on the phone as a "fire tsunami." He compared the Woolsey Fire to Category-5 events like Hurricane Katrina or Superstorm Sandy.

"I can't believe how people are talking about this," he said as we shook hands. "We got people out of harm's way. Tragic as their deaths were, we had only three people die. The *LA Times* is putting us in a bad light."

I was worried Pena was going to paint me with that brush, but then he added, "I liked your piece though."

Perhaps because the editor at the *Los Angeles Times* had removed any mention of why I'd ignored the mandatory evacuation order. For years, long-time locals like my friend, Tim Davis, had warned me there would be no firefighters when the fire came. It turned out they were right. But the *Times* didn't want to seem to be advocating "stay and defend" tactics. As a result, my Op-Ed made no mention of the lack of firefighters on the morning of November 9.

"I don't understand why people are so upset," Pena continued. "This was the biggest evacuation we've ever done. And 250,000 people were moved to safety. I understand some of the folks were upset about how much time it took but I've waited three hours to get out of sporting events."

I reminded him that people weren't complaining about being inconvenienced. Many were afraid they were going to be burned alive in their cars. Since the canyon roads were shut down, only one way out remained: down a gridlocked Pacific Coast Highway.

"We could have done better," Pena admitted referring to the upwards of six hours of gridlock. Some residents had reported sitting on the highway for eight hours. "We wanted to get all four lanes open into Santa Monica. We did at times, but it wasn't enough."

City council member Laura Rosenthal was on the PCH Task Force. She told me that all four lanes were open only briefly. She described how difficult it was to get the agencies involved, which included the California Highway Patrol and Cal-Trans, to talk to each other. In researching past fires, I learned that the PCH was gridlocked in the 1993 fire as well. Back then, too, the highway wasn't opened to allow more lanes running south into Santa Monica. In twenty-five years, it appears these agencies still haven't figured out how to open the highway during an emergency.

But what I really wanted to know was how the fire had gotten out of control in the first place. Pena said the fire started Thursday at approximately 2:30 p.m. on the former Rocketdyne site in Ventura County, now owned by Boeing. The rocky area was part of a mutual threat zone and covered jointly by three agencies: LA County Fire, Ventura County Fire, and LA City Fire. Because the Ventura County Fire Department was already overwhelmed fighting the nearby Hill Fire, which had started half an hour earlier, they sent few resources. Indeed, the Hill Fire was initially deemed to be the greater threat. It hopped the 101 Freeway almost immediately but soon began to run into areas burned in the 2013 Spring Fire. Due to the lack of fuel, the fire began to stall.

The Woolsey Fire was the opposite.

Because it started in the late afternoon, firefighters were only able to get two drops from fixed-wing aircraft before it got dark. The fixed-wing planes "paint" the fire with a red retardant to create control lines and prevent it from spreading.

"We felt if we could keep the fire to ten acres or less, we'd have a ninety percent chance of containing it," Pena said. "Once fires spread out, they're difficult, if not impossible, to control."

But with darkness grounding the planes, the fire began to grow. Firehawk helicopters ran all night making drops, but the fire gained momentum as it moved from the relatively flat area of Rocketdyne toward the canyons.

Additional resources were ordered, but the Woolsey Fire was third in line behind the Camp and Hill Fires and considered the lowest priority.

"If we had six more Firehawks, we could've stopped it," he said.

By 5:30 a.m. Friday, the fire had crossed the 101 Freeway in the Liberty Canyon area, where the freeway is brush on both sides, making it easier for flames to cross. The winds were blowing hard out of the northeast, pushing the fire into the corridor between Kanan and Decker canyons, which hadn't burned since 1978. Mature, twenty-foot-tall vegetation covered the area. The fire began its race toward the ocean.

"We knew once the fire hopped the 101 that life was going to be the priority," said Pena.

Shortly thereafter, the mandatory evacuation order was issued at 7:30 a.m.

Because of the fire's speed, LA County Fire had little chance to prep and defend. Instead, due to the size of the fire as well as their limited resources, they would have to use a fire front following strategy. Once the initial firestorm passed through, their engines and men would go in.

The problem with this was twofold.

First, many homes were destroyed when the firestorm came through. Secondly, due to the high winds, which hit seventy miles per hour, hundreds of power poles were snapped. A box truck was toppled over. Power lines littered the roads. The main canyon road into western Malibu, Kanan Dume, was shut down entirely.

"It looked like King Kong had come through," said Pena.

While the electric company, Southern California Edison, had shut off the power, no one knew whether lines on the road were still live and would present a threat to life. Firefighters are trained never to cross downed lines. This meant that many homes in Malibu were now inaccessible.

Normally, in advance of Santa Ana wind events, firefighting resources would shift from northern California to be staged further south. But this time, due to the Camp Fire in Paradise, no additional help from the north would be arriving. The LA County Fire Department put out a call for help from nearby cities. Many of the firefighters who came into Malibu from elsewhere, however, seemed less willing to fight the fire. There were numerous reported incidents of firefighters refusing to engage or of engines sitting idly by.

"But I bet they weren't wearing this patch," he said, pointing at the LA County Fire Department insignia on his sleeve.

He was right. For the most part, they weren't.

But residents didn't care where a firefighter came from. They weren't looking at patches on shirt sleeves. They wanted firefighters to save—or *try to save*—their homes. Reva Feldman had said she was "shocked" to hear the stories of firefighter indifference. As for the claims of some that they were "waiting for orders," Feldman said the firefighters she knew would put helping *before* orders.

"It's hard to come into this area," said Pena. "And this was as bad as we get. We can't have the same expectations on people coming from outside areas."

He said firefighters from outside areas didn't have the same level of training or confidence when it came to fighting brushfires. I shared with Pena the interaction Malibu City Council member Mikke Pearson had with firefighters who wouldn't even get out of their engine to assess.

"Unless it's something egregious, I'm comfortable with them not engaging," said Pena. "We don't want somebody from some outside city coming to our territory and getting hurt."

I wasn't sure what could be more egregious than a fire captain refusing to get out of his engine to assess a situation. Pierson and his son had been fighting the fire in Malibu West for hours with far less protective equipment and gear. They certainly had less training.

"Do you want to know what Berl Dahlstrom said when I told him that story?" I asked. Dahlstrom had been Pena's first training captain and was like a father to him.

"What did Berl say?"

"Are you sure you want to know?"

Pena nodded reluctantly.

"He called them cowards."

Pena winced. "I'm sure he did."

"He said if you didn't get out of your engine to evaluate you weren't doing your job."

It's a job firefighters are paid well to do. Malibu City Council member and Fire Captain Rick Mullen had been the subject of an *LA Times* front page exposé which documented his yearly income at $400,000, over half of which was in overtime. Berl said Osby should be *seeking out* those who'd experienced firefighters refusing to engage. Instead, the fire department, at first, denied such events even occurred.

Pena's concern about firefighters getting hurt or being killed, particularly those from outside the area, is understandable. He brought up the name of Glendale firefighter Bill Jensen, who was severely burned in the '96 Calabasas Fire. He worried that other agencies might not heed the mutual aid call in the future, should a firefighter from outside LA County die in Malibu.

"We had a city right next door not send anybody," he said, as evidence that other departments didn't want to put their firefighters at risk.

"Oxnard?"

"No, other direction."

"Pacific Palisades?"

"No, that's LA City Fire."

When I seemed stymied, Pena gave me a clue. "It has a pier."

"Hermosa Beach? Redondo?"

He shook his head as if he couldn't believe I wasn't getting it. Finally, I did.

"Santa Monica?"

He nodded. In my wildest dreams, I would never have imagined that Santa Monica wouldn't come to Malibu's aid. The cities share a long history, as well as a school district. Malibu was attempting to separate from Santa Monica and form its own school district, a process Santa Monica was resisting. They insisted on being paid "alimony" for fifty years to allow the "divorce" to go through. Yet, while the Santa Monica school board wanted Malibu's money, their fire department apparently wanted no part of fighting there during the worst fire in LA County history.

In fairness, calls for mutual aid are historically one-sided. Firefighters from LA County aren't being called into outside areas the way those firefighters are being called into Malibu. Wildfires are an all-too-regular occurrence, and they seem to be getting worse, a fact Pena wanted acknowledged. His department was taking the heat for the number of homes lost, which was close to 1,000 in the Malibu areas, but he felt that other agencies were equally responsible for the devastation. He wondered why the water department had no backup generators to keep their tanks pumping and full of water. Many neighborhoods, like mine, had no water. In neighborhoods that did have water, like Point Dume, the pressure was weak. He wanted more tanks with larger capacities, but he would settle for the tanks to work during a fire.

"The water department comes out like saints," he said. "I'm not buying it."

I wasn't either.

Mark Pestrella is the director of LA County Public Works, which includes the water department and other divisions like transportation, waste, construction, and emergency services. Pestrella says his organization is the largest public works agency in the US. He also claimed his department kept water in all the hydrants during the Woolsey Fire. But the fire hydrant at my house lost water on the morning of November 9. Fire Captain Ed Smith tried other hydrants in my neighborhood and found them dry as well. When I interviewed Pestrella and mentioned this, he said he would need to investigate the situation but never followed up.

Pena also expressed frustration with the power company, Southern California Edison, which appeared to be responsible for starting yet another major wildfire. Dozens of lawsuits had already been filed alleging exactly that. In the days after the fire, instead of replacing the nearly 2,000 downed power poles with steel ones, the power company simply used wood again.

Pena explained how much time had been wasted trying to get resources into Malibu during the fire. Kanan Dume Road was the major thoroughfare that led into western Malibu, but it was closed due to the fallen poles. Resources had to be detoured down Malibu Canyon road, which had steel poles, and then up the PCH, an additional forty minutes of drive time. Multiply that number by every trip first responders made, and an astronomical amount of time was lost; time that firefighters could have been saving homes. At the very least, Pena believed the poles on Kanan Dume Road should have been replaced with steel ones.

After the failure of the water company to provide ample water and the power company to provide equipment that didn't start fires, Pena saved some of his harshest criticism for homeowners.

"It's insanity, the number of trees these people have. The ornamentals killed us," he said, referring to the proliferation of highly flammable, non-native trees like pine, palm, and eucalyptus. Numerous people had more than a few flammable trees; they had *groves* of them, many over a hundred feet tall. No one should lose their home because of someone else's trees, but it happened repeatedly in the Woolsey Fire.

"Eucs are the worst thing out there," Pena said. "Their embers are aerodynamically designed to fly up to twenty-five miles. One ember can start a fire miles away."

He suggested homeowners have goats in their yards to eat the brush, something James Cameron did. The *Titanic* director certainly knows a thing or two about disasters. Pena also called out President Trump and the federal government for not maintaining the brush on their land. Twenty-five percent of the acreage that burned during the fire was National Park Service land. Yet days after the fire, President Trump called out California in a tweet, "There is no reason for these massive, deadly, and costly forest fires in California except that forest management is so poor."

Clearly, there were many parties to the catastrophe of the Woolsey Fire. Even if more firefighters had been willing to assist, many homes would still have been lost. I assured Pena I would do my part in voicing his concerns about areas for improvement in other departments, but I also wanted to know what his department would do differently.

"You're not going to find another agency that could do any better," he said. "We had helicopters flying forty out of forty-eight hours. A disaster is a disaster. This was a perfect storm. When the fire hopped the 101, it was like New Orleans when the levee broke."

Pena said the fire department would be doing an After Action Review (AAR) which would analyze what they could have done differently. Perhaps they would do more mutual aid training to get outside firefighters more comfortable in wildfire situations. But, again and again, Pena went back to this being a one percent fire, one we might not see again in our lifetimes.

While I wanted to believe him, I couldn't.

In 2018, California had deadly fires in Malibu and Paradise. In 2017, it was Santa Rosa and Ventura. Four of the ten most destructive fires in the state's history have occurred within the last two years. With climate change, it seems likely California (and other western states) will have more of these extreme fires, not fewer.

With all due respect to Pena, every agency, every elected official, and every homeowner needs to do far better in the future. Otherwise, next time—and there will be a next time—many more people will die. Homeowners, for the most part, continue to ignore the risks of living in what Pena called "one of the most disaster-centric places" on earth. Besides being the wildfire capital of North America, two sizable earthquakes with hundreds of aftershocks occurred in July 2019, reminding residents that the "Big One" was still out there. With the world getting hotter and ocean levels rising, the coastline is eroding as well, which increases the risk of flooding too.

But most homeowners don't want to deal with any of those issues. Instead of proactively planning for the next catastrophe that will strike, they want the government to rescue them when reality smacks them in the face—or catches their pine trees on fire. But governmental agencies aren't set up to deviate from protocol. They often fail in emergencies, when deviating is exactly what's needed.

This means homeowners should take responsibility and be prepared *before* the next fire or earthquake (or tsunami) hits. Get a fire pump, hoses, retardants, and protective gear. Build a water tank while you're at it. Set up a generator.

Stock up on food, water, and medicines. It's not doomsday advice but simple common sense.

There is hope, for it seems that some people have gotten the memo.

My across-the-street neighbor lived in a forest of flammable trees, so it was no shock when his house burned to the ground. What surprised me was that afterwards he cut down every tree on his property, even the ones that hadn't burned. He learned his lesson, but many other homeowners stubbornly refuse to remove dangerous trees, claiming they create privacy and add value to their homes. But what's the value of a burned-down house?

By clearing your brush, you give yourself, your neighbors, and the fire department a fighting chance. I wonder how many homeowners would remove their flammable trees if firefighters said they would no longer defend such properties.

Experts I interviewed said the most important thing homeowners can do to mitigate the fire risk is to reduce the amount of available fuel. Yet more than six months after I begged members of the Malibu City Council to institute a flammable landscaping and materials ordinance, nothing has been done.

Living in California, for all its beauty and great weather, means being only a natural disaster away from living on the streets. Some people believe it was folly to build in Malibu in the first place, let alone to rebuild over and over. But are those same people saying we shouldn't build in New Orleans or in Florida or in Tornado Alley? The true folly is to rebuild without making any changes.

To my knowledge, the city of Malibu hasn't instituted a single law to make Malibu more fire safe.

Example of leaning and deteriorated SCE pole in Malibu Canyon, one of which was responsible for starting the 2007 Canyon Fire.

PHOTO HANS LAETZ

22

FIRESTARTERS

Southern California Edison is one of the nation's largest electric utilities with roots that go back more than a hundred years. A subsidiary of Edison International, the Rosemead-based company serves a 50,000-square-mile area covering much of central and southern California that includes 15 million residents. A privately owned public utility, SCE enjoys a state-protected monopoly, holds more than $50 million in assets, and regularly posts enviable, if regulated, profits.

Over the last quarter-century, SCE has also posted some less-flattering numbers.

Since 1993, the utility has caused or contributed to seven massive California wildfires: Mill Creek Fire, Riverside County Fire, Stearns Wharf Fire, Big Creek Forest Fire, Malibu's Canyon Fire, Night Sky Fire, and the San Bernardino National Forest Fire. In the past decade alone, SCE has paid nearly $100 million in settlements and verdicts. In March 2019, investigators finally determined that SCE power lines were responsible for igniting the Thomas Fire that burned through Ventura and Santa Barbara Counties in late 2017, killing two and creating the conditions for mudslides that killed another twenty-one people a month later (SCE pushed back on the report's conclusions). Combined insurance claims on those two tragedies alone total around $1.7 billion. If any entity knows how expensive—in dollars, reputation, and often lives—California wildfires can be, it is Southern California Edison.

The early days of November 2018 in and around Los Angeles were especially hot and windy, prompting the National Weather Service to put out a red flag warning for high fire risk in the area. On November 6, two days before the Woolsey Fire, SCE activated its Emergency Operations Center and began its notification program, which warned customers, fire chiefs, and governmental agencies that, because of the extreme fire danger, "27,000 customers are being notified of possible power shutoffs." The idea was to turn off the power before Santa Ana winds damaged their equipment or knocked down power lines, either one of which could start a fire. Authorities appeared to be prepared, and the stage was preemptively set to protect against any major problems.

According to California Department of Forestry and Fire Protection, the state's firefighting organization, the Woolsey Fire started on Thursday, November 8, at 2:24 p.m. in Simi Valley at the Santa Susana Field Laboratory site (SSFL), a property owned by Boeing. Two minutes prior, SCE had reported an outage with its Big Rock circuit at the Chatsworth substation in the old Rocketdyne facility located on the SSFL site. Immediately afterward, flames were sighted in Woolsey Canyon near that location.

Yet SCE did not proactively "de-energize" or shut off power to any of its customers. If it had, as it warned it was going to, yet another catastrophic wildfire might have been avoided. All SCE had to do was flip the proverbial switch. Instead, the Woolsey Fire was given time to bite into the overgrown, poisoned vegetation at Santa Susana. The winds then propelled it across 100,000 acres of land, causing more than $6 billion in damage and losses. The fire would eventually destroy 2,000 structures, force nearly 300,000 people to evacuate, injure several firefighters, and kill three people.

Anthony Baklayan and his mother, Shoushan, were among them.

"We lost *everything.*" That is what many people I interviewed in this book told me. Most of them were referring to material possessions—homes, heirlooms, cars, clothes—but the sentiment also includes the damage done to memories, pride, and emotional security. By these standards, many of them certainly had lost "everything." But for Terri Baklayan the statement carries an additional, unfathomable dimension. Terri lost more than a collection of keepsakes and a few cars. She lost her husband of thirty years—the love of her life.

Terri and Anthony, along with two of their three adult children, slept at her mother-in-law Shoushan's home on Mulholland Highway in northern Malibu on the night of Thursday, November 8. They'd been forced to evacuate their own home in Oak Park, which is only about four miles southwest of the Santa Susana site, when the flames got too close. But the fire followed them, pushing another five miles south, crossing the 101 Freeway.

On Friday, the full force of the Woolsey Fire came down into the Mulholland area. Along the way, thick, dry chaparral that hadn't burned in forty years increased the speed, intensity, and heat of the flames. With the Santa Anas blasting, these wildfires could move so quickly that it was sometimes hard for residents to judge its distance. The older and drier brush was, the hotter and faster it burned. The Baklayan family scrambled to collect their things and get away once they realized the menacing reality of the situation.

In the chaos, Anthony rushed to get his elderly mother into one of their cars and started to drive her out. But the thick smoke, which was already smothering the neighborhood, was disorienting. He followed a fire engine he believed was heading to safety, but then saw, too late, that it was moving directly toward the fire to save homes. Anthony attempted to turn around, but flames leapt from the side of the road, engulfing his car. Huddled together inside, he and his mother were swallowed whole by the flames.

The coroner marked the cause of death as "thermal injuries," which is a delicate way of saying that Anthony and Shoushan's bodies had been incinerated. Terri managed to escape with minor burn injuries, and one of her sons suffered smoke inhalation. All three family cars were destroyed.

Given her tragic losses, I was nervous about reaching out to Terri and her children. Instead, I called Anthony's brother, Steve, who hadn't been present during those horrific final moments. A quiet man who kept things "bottled up," Steve had lost his mother and only sibling, and he was having a hard time dealing with the tragedy. Though kind and respectful when I called him, he wasn't willing to say much. Later, he texted me that he "wasn't ready to talk." I was prepared to give up on telling Anthony and Shoushan's story when Terri contacted me.

She wanted their story told, but wanted it told correctly by someone who had been there. She believed that sharing it would be therapeutic and wanted to process her grief in a way that was helpful to her and to others. She felt strongly that expressing painful emotions caused by the fire's trauma would alleviate future psychological distress. It was important to her that Anthony and Shoushan be mentioned in the book, along with the other casualty of the Woolsey Fire, Dr. Alfred De Ciutiis, a retired oncologist, known as "Dr. D." He was trapped in his home by the flames and also died of thermal injuries.

Terri agreed to meet with me, then cancelled the meeting. She said she wanted to tell me the story of what happened that day but ultimately decided she couldn't. She had filed a multimillion-dollar wrongful death suit, and as a legal secretary she knew speaking to me could cause complications or damage her case. She was sure her attorney wouldn't approve of it, and I couldn't argue with her. She had been robbed of something precious and incalculable, and the last thing I wanted was to negatively impact her potential for legal remedy.

But I had to ask, "Who is on the receiving end of the suit?"

"Southern California Edison," Terri said.

Malibu super-lawyer Peter McNulty and his firm, McNulty Law, are among the nearly one hundred lawyers and law firms suing SCE in the wake of the Woolsey Fire. In a mass tort filing, he represents more than 200 plaintiffs, many of whom he knows personally from having lived in Malibu for twenty-five years. (He does not represent Terri Baklayan and her family.)

This is far from the first large civil action against SCE.

Malibu resident Hans Laetz sued SCE (and five cell phone companies) for starting the 2007 Canyon Fire, claiming that they had illegally overloaded old power poles on Malibu Canyon Road in a way that caused them to fail in the powerful Santa Ana winds. As part of the settlement, SCE and the cell companies paid $66.7 million in fines and penalties, half of which was used for repairs of various sorts. The decrepit Malibu Canyon poles, which had been the source of not one but two major fires were thus, finally, replaced. Laetz, who now runs the local radio station, KBUU, spent eight years of his life on that case in the face of SCE's intransigence.

McNulty said that the dirty secret is that it's cheaper for SCE to fight—and lose—lawsuits than to spend the money necessary to make their poles and equipment safer. After all, how many Hans Laetzes—everyday people willing to invest so much of their own time and money to fight these battles—were out there?

I reached out by phone to J. Christopher Thompson, SCE's VP of Local Affairs for Southern California, to find out why the company hadn't immediately shut off the power at the Chatsworth substation given the warnings of extreme fire conditions. Chris was apprehensive but open to setting up an interview. A few days later, though, he followed up with a curt text *In consultation with my communications team, we are going to pass on the opportunity.*

I've made more than 200 interview requests in the six months of writing this book, and SCE remains the only entity or individual that has refused to speak with me.

McNulty speculated that it's because SCE knows it's liable since it had ignored the wind and fire conditions, as well as its own safety protocol. SCE could be negligent, too, for failing to maintain safe electrical facilities and perform vegetation management to reduce brush around its equipment. In his court filing, McNulty spells out this accusation clearly:

> *California wildfires caused by unsafe, ineffective, and dated utility company equipment have been occurring for decades. Prior to the devastating Woolsey Fire, SCE had been fined multiple times over the past three decades for their repeated failure to ensure the safety of their equipment and for failing to take necessary measures to mitigate the risk of wildfires in their service areas. The responsibility of utility companies ensuring the safety of their equipment is extremely important as wildfires caused by their equipment are generally widespread, fast moving, and devastating. The history of fines levied against SCE since 1993 exposes their reckless conduct and indifference to the residents of California.*

Given the legal actions, SCE has little incentive to talk publicly about its purported role in the fire and every reason to avoid risking an admission of fault.

McNulty also considers Boeing, which owns the Santa Susana Field Laboratory, responsible since it failed to perform vegetation management on the nearly 3,000-acre site, negligence that enabled the fire to get out of control quickly. Boeing didn't even have fire suppression personnel or equipment in place to prevent the type of fire that could reasonably be anticipated in those conditions. If it had, the fire could have been put out right away. Not only did the fire burn through the Santa Monica Mountains, as well as Los Angeles and Ventura Counties, it burned through the Santa Susana Nuclear complex—the same complex where, in 1959, a nuclear reactor suffered the worst nuclear disaster in United States history. Boeing, although responsible to do so, had failed to remediate the radioactive nuclear materials and other toxic contaminates in the soil and vegetation on the site. Those contaminates had been scattered by the hurricane force winds throughout the fire zone. Radioactive materials like cesium-139, strontium-90, and plutonium-239 had gone from being somewhat contained on 3,000 acres to potentially spreading anywhere within the 100,000 acres the fire burned.

Anthony Noubar Baklayan's extended family held a memorial service at the Viewpoint School in Calabasas, not far from where the fire claimed him. Terri and their kids—Thomas, Susie, and Todd—were there, along with Anthony's brother, Steve, and his children, Chelsea, Stephanie, and Cheyenne. Together, with more than 700 people who had known Anthony, they paid respects to their husband, father, brother, uncle. Anthony was fifty-seven years old when he died.

Terri sent me the program from the memorial service and the nearly hour-long video recorded during the event. She wanted me to know that Anthony was "a good man" and the "light of her life." I found myself often staring at his picture in the program—he's wearing a crisp collared shirt and tie, a hint of amusement teasing at his upper lip—since he looked so much like my Uncle Jack. They had the same bushy hair and dark eyes, the same warm smile and thick eyebrows —teddy bears come to life.

This isn't as strange as it sounds. Anthony and I both come from Armenian stock, though I am not full blooded. (My family's name was originally Kerbeckian; Armenian names end with *-ian,* or as in Anthony's case, *-yan*). Our ancestors had fled the Turks and the Armenian Genocide of 1915, during which an estimated two million of our brethren were murdered. These survivors escaped but were stripped of everything they owned, often walking hundreds of miles on foot to find safe haven. Many died in search of a new home. As a result, like drifting sparks from a fire, Armenians were scattered across the world.

Anthony's father, Noubar, was born in Cairo and lived to be ninety years old, which gives us a sense of how long Anthony might have lived had the fire not taken his life. His mother Shoushan was born in Jerusalem. She was eighty-two at the time of her death. I know from my own experience how fierce Armenian family loyalties are. My father would have done anything for his mother, as I would for mine. Once, as a boy, I said something negative about my grandmother. With more than a hint of violence, my father told me never to make that mistake again.

At the memorial service, the eulogy was given by Steve Brooks, an elder in the West Woodland Hills congregation of Jehovah's Witnesses. Brooks explained how Anthony had begun to study the *Bible* in his late teens and eventually was baptized as one of Jehovah's Witnesses in 1980. Anthony spent more than thirty years volunteering as an elder, preparing and sharing *Bible* talks, and traveling to other congregations to speak. He was also active in field service, which meant knocking on the doors of strangers to spread the word of God.

Brooks told the story of how Terri and Anthony met and fell in love in 1988. They both were coming out of relationships in which their partners had been unfaithful. In the *Bible*, Paul says, "we've grown together in pain," and this became an apt description of how the couple connected and flourished. Anthony and Terri were married for more than three decades, and according to Brooks, not a day went by without Anthony telling Terri that he loved her. As if the loss of a love like that wasn't devastating enough, Terri had witnessed most of the event. She had barely escaped with her own life. At one point, she thought she had lost her youngest son only to find out later that it was actually her husband who was gone.

How do you go on from that, let alone recover?

Over six months after the fire, I spoke with Terri when she was on the way to get her hair done, something she hadn't done since her husband's death.

"I'm trying not to let myself go," she said, as if she felt guilty for spending a moment on herself. "I'm doing my best not to hold things in."

She took solace in knowing that Anthony had tried to protect his mother, that he had died showing the greatest love any human being can show for another.

In Loving Memory of
ANTHONY BAKLAYAN
April 15th, 1961 – November 9th, 2018

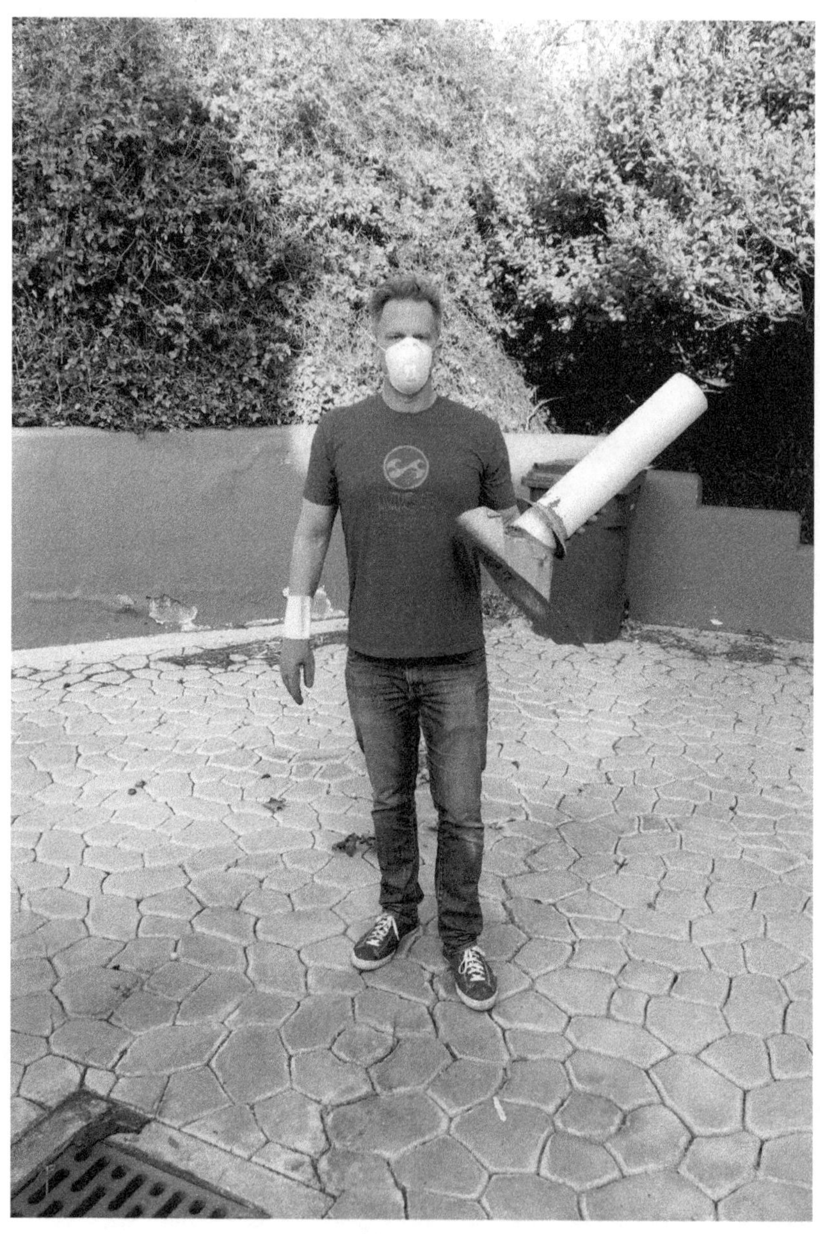

Our home survived, but parts of our roof did not.
PHOTO DAVIS KERBECK

EPILOGUE

MALIBU FIRE GUY

It took me a long time to go surfing again after the Woolsey Fire burned most of my Malibu Park neighborhood to the ground. Normally, I surfed a couple of times a week, often with my son, Davis. In the twenty-five years since I moved from New York to Santa Monica, I don't think I've gone more than a week without crashing some waves. I wouldn't survive without the release the sport—and the ocean—gives me.

I hadn't done much to alleviate my stress about the fire other than writing the Op-Ed for the *Los Angeles Times*. Being out on the water, I hoped, would set me on a course for recovery, so I grabbed a stand-up surfboard from our hotel's surf locker. We—my wife, Gardia, Davis, and I—had recently checked into the Malibu hotel after spending three weeks evacuated to my mother's home over the hill in nearby Thousand Oaks. At first, we thought we were doing our insurance company a favor by not making them pay for a hotel, that perhaps this would make them get an adjustor out to our home sooner to assess the damage and begin the clean-up, but we couldn't even get an appointment. I hoped that seeing hotel bills might speed up the process.

I lugged the heavy SUP board down the stairs to their beach. The coolest thing about the hotel—besides the fact that it didn't burn down—was its proximity to the ocean. Waves smashed directly into the hotel, shaking the building. At night, the surf was so loud that Gardia, Davis, and I had trouble sleeping, though that was also a result of what we'd been through.

At the water's edge, I hopped onto the board and paddled toward the Malibu Pier. It felt good to be out on the water, though I noticed enormous fields of debris. An unusually large early rain had flushed out the creek beds. The water close to shore was the color of chocolate but I didn't care. Farther out, shredded and burned pieces of material—from trees that had exploded, houses demolished, God knew what else—littered the water, clinging to my board, the waves unable to filter the wreckage that now tainted the Pacific. I paddled under the pier and through the pilings, which gave me a bit of an adrenaline rush, something I hadn't felt since fighting the fire.

Once through the pier, I saw the crowd out at Surfrider, one of the best waves in the world. Made famous by the 1959 movie *Gidget,* which took place at Surfrider beach, the wave spawned hundreds of surf films, surf music, and a surf culture which continues to this day. Normally, there are over a hundred ultra-competitive surfers in the water, many of them pros. But nothing was normal in Malibu in those first weeks after the fire. That day, hardly anyone was surfing. The last time the crowd was this light might have been the weekend before *Gidget* was released.

In my twenty years living in Malibu, I'd only surfed Surfrider a handful of times. I couldn't handle the crowds. Surfers are not known for being a friendly bunch. They especially don't like to share their waves.

"What do you guys talk about while you're out there?" my mother once asked me.

"Uh, we don't talk to each other."

"All that time waiting for waves and you don't say *anything* to the person sitting right next to you?"

"Nope, never."

I realized if you weren't a surfer, you didn't know about surfers jockeying for position and cutting each other off. You didn't know about leash pulling or stink eye or being sounded (yelled at) in the water. If you were going to get into a fight in Malibu, Surfrider was the place. Many locals have surfed there all their lives and feel like they own the waves. They don't hesitate to tell a new face what to do, which usually means "Get the fuck out of the water."

Though the crowd was small, ten or fifteen people, I reminded myself to tread lightly. I was on a large stand-up board, which made it easier for me to catch waves and make other surfers jealous—or piss them off. Sometimes the regular surfers would get into it with the stand-up guys. Many felt that SUP boards should be banned altogether. Fortunately, there were a couple of other guys out on stand-up boards so I wasn't the only one.

Usually, the surf at Surfrider wasn't as good in the winter months, but on this December day it was chest high and perfect. I paddled into the pack and found myself stroking for the first wave I saw, despite the voice in my head admonishing me to let one of those who'd been waiting get the wave.

I'd instantly succumbed to the siren call of riding a wave.

I caught the wave and rode it for what seemed like an eternity, at least the length of a football field. By the end, my legs were shaky; I was out of surfing shape. Still, I rode the wave practically to the sand. On the way back out, I noticed another stand-up paddler behind me. He was a big guy of about fifty. Had he been on the same wave as me? If so, I'd dropped in front of him, a big no-no in the surfing world. I'd been so excited to surf my first wave in over a month that I hadn't bothered to check behind me to see if someone else had caught the wave, which would make it "theirs."

I gave him a little hand wave by way of an apology. I certainly wasn't going to say anything out loud and break the silence. I just wanted to let him know it was an accident and that I knew better. I was so happy to be surfing, hell, to be alive, I'd let my exuberance get the better of me.

"No problem, bro," I imagined him saying. "We Malibu people got to stick together after what we've been through."

Instead, the dude glared at me.

To be safe, I kept my distance as we paddled back out. When we reached the lineup again, he paddled over to a young man, who was also on a stand-up board. They whispered together and then looked my way.

Uh-oh.

I let a bunch of good waves go through—staying where I was—so everyone out had a chance to catch something. Then I spotted a medium-sized wave with no one on it. I paddled for the wave but as I did, the young man also paddled for it, which was strange since it was far from the best wave of the day. There were plenty of other waves rolling through, especially for a strong young guy on a stand-up board.

He put himself in position for the wave to be his—even though I'd taken off for the wave long before him. I looked back to check this time and saw him catch the wave, which meant I had to let him have it. He flew down the line in front of me, but instead of enjoying the wave, he gave me a dirty look.

Yup, stink eye.

Getting into it with a couple of surfers was the last thing I needed. I decided I'd let the guys get their waves and then once they were inside, I would be free to grab whichever wave I wanted. The problem with my strategy was that the two men didn't play along. Each time they saw me go for a wave, one of them went for it too, aggressively paddling to get in position behind me. When one of them took off, the other waited in the lineup watching me to see what wave I would go for. They'd wait for me to commit and then start paddling to steal the wave.

I'd gone surfing to find some peace from the memories of the fire, but now, with the men seemingly angling for trouble, I just wanted to avoid having my ass kicked. Many a brawl had begun with an incident like mine. Often, the bad blood made it to the beach where the two guys would have at it. I'd seen one fight. The surfers hammered each other until one went down. I don't think the police were even called. Malibu has a reputation of being the home of the rich and famous but it is still, to this day, the Wild West.

I realized the only thing I could do to avoid a fight—or catch any waves—was to apologize, which meant I had to talk. The two men were doing circles around me, getting wave after wave, while I stood there gathering the courage to speak. I decided to start with the older guy.

"Hey man," I said as he was paddling back after another great ride. "You're killing it there on the inside." I figured a little flattery never hurt.

He pretended he didn't hear me, though his annoyance was real. "What?"

"You and your son are killing it. You're getting some great waves."

"He's not my son," he said with a sneer.

If things kept going in this direction, we'd be clubbing each other with our paddles any second. I looked down, trying to get the courage to swallow my pride and apologize, when I saw the shingle of a roof floating in front of me. The recent rains had washed the remains of burned-down homes into the sea.

"Look at that," I said. "It's someone's roof."

"Yeah," the guy said, but I did get him to look.

"Heavy." I started to choke up, which took me by surprise. I didn't want this man to see that—or to know what I'd been through.

"Probably from the houses west of here," he said, gesturing in the direction of my home. "Current brought them down this way. We lost a lot of homes in Malibu, some are saying close to a thousand."

"Yeah, I almost lost mine."

Up until this point, the guy hadn't looked at me once. He kept staring out toward the waves, ready to bolt the second he saw a good one, but now he took me in before quickly looking away again.

"You live here?" he asked, his eyes searching the surf.

"Yeah, Malibu Park."

"Shit, that was ground zero. Not many made it."

"I know. I wrote an article about it for the *Los Angeles Times*."

The man glared at me as if I'd wasted enough of his time.

"Hey," I said, "I didn't mean to cut you off on that—"

"Wait a second, you're that guy," he said, actually looking me in the eyes. "The fire guy."

"What? No, I just wrote an essay."

"Yeah, in the *LA Times*. I read it. It was called the Malibu fire guy, right?"

"Uh, no, it was called 'The Accidental Firefighter.'"

"Yeah, that's it. The Accidental Firefighter. Holy shit, dude. Your wife is a badass. She saved your house."

I wanted to say that my son and I had something to do with it, too, but his point was well taken. If it weren't for Gardia, our home would be gone.

"Hey," he yelled toward the young man. "Get over here."

The young man whipped his head around and started paddling like a maniac. The other surfers, too, started coming our way like they were going to witness a fight.

"This is the fire guy," he said when they were within earshot. "Remember the article I showed you about the guy who saved his house with his wife and kid? This is the guy!"

"Wow, dude, that was gnarly," the kid said. The frown he'd worn as he stole waves from me was replaced by a look of awe.

"I read that article," one of the other surfers who'd gathered around us chimed in. "Intense, man. Glad you made it."

"Uh, thanks." It struck me that no one was watching the surf. Wave after wave rolled through unridden.

"What was that chemical you used?" the older man asked.

"Phos-Chek."

"This guy had masks and firehoses and Phos-Chek. He saved his house from the worst fire in LA County history," he told the others, summing up the essay for those who hadn't read it. "His fire pump failed, but he had a special wrench to use the hydrant at the top of his street. His wife watched a YouTube video the night before to figure out how to use it." He glanced at me to make sure he was getting it right. Surfers sat on their boards like kids listening to a scary story at overnight camp.

"There were no firefighters at all, right?" he asked.

"I didn't see one," I said.

"Dude, you gotta write about that."

I shrugged. "I did."

"No, you wrote about how you survived. You gotta write about what *happened*. How things got so screwed up that your wife and son were doing the work firefighters should have been doing. You can tell the stories of locals saving neighborhoods all by themselves, of people saving hundreds of animals."

"Yeah, bro, you could write a movie," the kid said.

"Well, *Inside Edition* did want to put us on TV," I said, sheepishly. They had reached out after the article to interview me and my family, but it seemed wrong for us to brag about saving our home when, in a neighborhood of 275 homes, nearly 200 were gone.

"Fuck *Inside Edition*," the older man said, "and fuck a movie for that matter. You saved your house when hardly anyone did. You can teach people to be more prepared. You can help change things so that this doesn't happen again."

The surfers sitting around me nodded in agreement like some decision had been made.

"Lots of people stayed and fought the fire," I said. "Many of them for a lot longer than I did."

"Sorry, man, but you're the fire guy. You gotta do something with that. Pay tribute to those who did what they did. They represent the spirit of old Malibu, the spirit that resides in all of us. We just have to let it guide us. Not only in disasters, man, but every fucking day."

Inwardly I smiled. The guy had grown philosophical from the soapbox of his stand-up board, but he had a point. Locals I didn't know had stopped at my home to prevent stray embers from burning it to the ground. Had I not tracked them down, I never even would've known who they were. They didn't ask for a thing, not a bottle of wine, not a dinner out, not even acknowledgement.

I spotted a bump on the horizon, which meant a set was on its way. From the size of the bump, it looked like the biggest set of the day. The town hall meeting broke up as surfers scrambled to get into position to grab one of the waves.

As the older man paddled off, he said, "Nice surfing with you, fire guy."

Though we weren't really surfing together. I'd had only one wave the entire session, but if I could help anyone understand what had happened on November 9 and do anything to prevent future catastrophes, perhaps that wave would turn out to be the most important one of my life.

Sifters were used to sort through the rubble to find anything that survived.

PHOTO ROBERT KERBECK

ACKNOWLEDGEMENTS

As I've portrayed in the preceding pages, the Woolsey Fire was the worst day of many peoples' lives. I want to thank those who allowed me to interview them, reliving the events that transpired so I could tell their stories. I am indebted to them and humbled by their courage and generosity. I would not have been able to write this book without their support, and for that, I offer my deepest thanks.

To those whose stories didn't make it into the book, it is by no means a reflection on you or your tales. They were every bit as worthy and I hope to tell them in the future.

In addition to those mentioned within the book I'd like to thank the following: Kyle Grillot, Kirby and Honore Kotler, Jay Thorson, Lyn Christensen, Jack and Vonnie Street, Sharan Street, Seth Kramer, Rebel Steiner, Laurel Thorne, Greg Cooper, Tracy Vail, Jeff Stockwell, Barbara Osborn, Sheila Kuehl, Adam Wolfson, Tim Davis, Mary Long, Gigi Goyette, Sean Butler, Teresa Earle, Dan Bercu, Jon Klane, Scully Cloete, Karen Farrer, Skyler Peak, Janice Burns, Daniel Ralston, Rick Wallace, Adam Rocke, Tiffany Hawk, Jennifer Brody, Zach Powers, Sally Shore, Brendan Spiegel, Jasmine Alkouri, Laura Espinoza, Jay Fernandez, SJ Main Muñoz, Linda Immediato, Maer Roshan, Paul Grisanti, Conrad Romo, Ray Hartman, Beth Grossman, Carina Sammartino, Elle Bishop, and my agent, Dean Krystek.

Thanks go to Robin Rauzi at the *Los Angeles Times* for publishing "The Accidental Firefighter," which was the genesis of this book. I'd also like to thank Talmon Smith at the *New York Times* for asking me to write the piece in the first place.

Thank you to the many people who assisted with the editing of this book: Helga Schier, Yi Shun Lai, and members of the Malibu Writers Circle, including John Struloeff, Sandra Ramos O'Briant, Michal Lemberger, Naomi Eagleson, and Bridget Crocker. Extra credit goes to members Asher Sund and Liz Ziemska for reading some of these chapters again and again. I'd particularly like to thank my writing brother-in-arms, Michael Bland, for being there from the beginning, always with encouragement and superlative notes.

Finally, I'd like to thank my wife and son for being the best things that have ever happened to me—and pretty good firefighters to boot.

BIBLIOGRAPHY

"After Woolsey Fire Erupted, Impromptu Seagoing Support Team Piloted Supplies into Malibu." *Daily News*, 13 Nov. 2018, www.dailynews.com/2018/11/13/after-woolsey-fire-erupted-impromptu-seagoing-support-team-piloted-supplies-into-malibu/.

Bradley, Ian. "Https://www.theacorn.com/Articles/Coroner-Identifies-Woolsey-Fire-Victims/." *The Acorn*, 13 Dec. 2018, www.theacorn.com/articles/coroner-identifies-woolsey-fire-victims/.

Cagle, Kate. "LA County Could Expand On-Call Fire Program in Malibu." *Spectrum News 1*, Spectrum News 1, 8 Mar. 2019, spectrumnews1.com/ca/la-west/public-safety/2019/03/08/la-county-could-expand-on-call-fire-program-in-malibu#.

Collins, Michael. "Los Angeles, State Smack Back at Illegal Trump Plan to Kill SSFL Cleanup." *EnviroReporter*, EnviroReporter, 18 Feb. 2019, www.enviroreporter.com/2019/02/los-angeles-state-smack-back-at-illegal-trump-plan-to-kill-ssfl-cleanup/.

Cosgrove, Jaclyn. "Must Reads: Firefighters' Fateful Choices: How the Woolsey Fire Became an Unstoppable Monster." *Los Angeles Times*, 6 Jan. 2019, www.latimes.com/local/lanow/la-me-woolsey-resources-20190106-htmlstory.html.

Davis, Mike. *Ecology of Fear: Los Angeles and the Imagination of Disaster*. Verso Books, 1999.

Folkers, Cindy. "TRITIUM: HEALTH CONSEQUENCES." *NIRS*, Nuclear Information and Resource Service, 1 Apr. 2006, www.nirs.org/wp-content/uploads/factsheets/tritiumbasicinfo.pdf.

Hall, Marian, and Nick Rodionoff. *Malibu: California's Most Famous Seaside Community*. Angel City Press, 2005.

Halpern, Jake. "The Last of the Malibu Hillbillies." *LA Weekly*, 10 July 2003, www.laweekly.com/the-last-of-the-malibu-hillbillies/.

Harris, Mike. "Long-Planned Cleanup of Santa Susana Field Lab Delayed Again, Activists Disappointed." *Ventura County Star*, 21 Aug. 2018, www.vcstar.com/story/news/local/communities/simi-valley/2018/08/21/simi-valley-santa-susana-field-lab-cleanup-delayed-again-nuclear-meltdown/978261002/.

Hepler, Lauren. "California Reckons With the Cost of Wildfires to Come." *New York Times*, 7 June 2019, www.nytimes.com/2019/06/07/business/california-wildfire-commission.html?action=click&module=Top%20Stories&pgtype=Homepage.

Hirsch, Daniel. "Critique of DTSC 'Interim Summary' of Woolsey Fire 12-18-18." *Committee to Bridge the Gap*, Committee to Bridge the Gap, 18 Dec. 2018, committeetobridgethegap.org/wp-content/uploads/2018/12/CritiqueOfDTSC_Interim_Summary-Final.pdf.

Kamen, Ed. "Rising from the Ashes." *Malibu Times*, 9 May 2012, www.malibutimes.com/malibu_life/article_cf382cf7-8f4f-5c86-92d1-c6457b8cd0ca.html.

Macfadyen, William. "Malibu Woman Didn't Stand a Chance in Collision with Highway 101 Palm Tree." *Noozhawk*, 20 Oct. 2017, www.noozhawk.com/article/bill_macfadyen_malibu_woman_killed_highway_101_crash_santa_barbara_20171020.

"Malibu Magazine - After the Woolsey Fire." *Malibu Magazine - After the Woolsey Fire*, 1 Jan. 2019.

"Massive Woolsey Fire Began On Contaminated Santa Susana Field Laboratory, Close to Site of Partial Meltdown." *Physicians for Social Responsibility-Los Angeles*, Physicians for Social Responsibility-Los Angeles, 12 Nov. 2018, www.psr-la.org/massive-woolsey-fire-began-on-contaminated-santa-susana-field-laboratory-close-to-site-of-partial-meltdown/.

Meares, Hadley. "The History of How Malibu Grew." *Curbed LA*, Curbed LA, 21 Nov. 2018, la.curbed.com/2018/11/21/18098866/malibu-history-fire-development-growth-adamson.

Oswald, John A. "Talented Orchid Man Brings Beauty to Life in Malibu Laboratory." *Los Angeles Times*, 16 July 1988, www.latimes.com/archives/la-xpm-1988-07-16-me-5804-story.html.

Randall, David K. *The King and Queen of Malibu: The True Story of the Battle for Paradise*. W. W. Norton & Company, 2017.

"Report of the Santa Susana Field Laboratory Advisory Panel." Santa Susana Field Laboratory Advisory Panel, 1 Oct. 2006.

Rindge, Frederick Hastings. *Happy Days in Southern California*. BookFactory, 2017.

Schultz, Kathy Jean. "KIDS AND CANCER: Resident of Nearby Rocketdyne Shines Light on Unusual Diagnoses." *Ventura County Reporter*, 15 Aug. 2018, www.vcreporter.com/2018/08/kids-and-cancer-resident-of-nearby-rocketdyne-shines-light-on-unusual-diagnoses/.

Stiles, Matt, et al. "Malibu's Wildfire History." *Los Angeles Times*, 12 Dec. 2018, www.latimes.com/projects/la-me-malibu-wildfire-history/.

Stotsenberg, Dorothy D. *My Fifty Years in Malibu*. Pepperdine University Press, 2005.

"Trump Administration Breaks Agreement With California For Cleanup Of Nuclear Meltdown Site." *Committee to Bridge the Gap*, Committee to Bridge the Gap, 19 Dec. 2018, committeetobridgethegap.org/2018/12/19/trump-administration-breaks-agreement-with-california-for-cleanup-of-nuclear-meltdown-site/.

Virbila, S. Irene. "The Review: The Old Place." *Los Angeles Times*, 10 Feb. 2011, www.latimes.com/food/la-fo-review-20110210-story.html.

Walker, Alissa. "Why Pepperdine Stays Put When Wildfires Rage." *Curbed LA*, Curbed LA, 20 Nov. 2018, la.curbed.com/2018/11/20/18097889/wildfire-pepperdine-malibu-shelter-in-place.